DATE DUE

JUN 2 9 2005	
AUG 3 1 2005	
NOV 0 7 2005	
12/17	
DEC 2 6 2005	
MAY 7	

EMCO, INC. 38-2931

A DAVID & CHARLES BOOK

David & Charles is a subsidiary of F&W (UK) Ltd., an F&W Publications Inc. company

First published in the UK in 2004
Originally published as *1001 perles à broder, coller, enfiler* by Dessain et Tolra, France 2002

Distributed in North America
by F&W Publications, Inc.
4700 East Galbraith Road
Cincinnati, OH 45236
1-800-289-0963

A catalogue record for this book is available from the British Library.

ISBN 0 7153 1793 8 Paperback

Printed in China by SNP Leefung
for David & Charles
Brunel House Newton Abbot Devon

Visit our website at www.davidandcharles.co.uk

David & Charles books are available from all good bookshops; alternatively you can contact our Orderline on (0)1626 334555 or write to us at FREEPOST EX2110, David & Charles Direct, Newton Abbot, TQ12 4ZZ (no stamp required UK mainland).

1001 beads

Irène Lassus and Marie-Anne Voituriez

David & Charles

Contents

Key to symbols

The cost of each project is given beside the list of materials required for each project.

★ *Easy* — *Inexpensive*

★★ *Moderate* — *Reasonable*

★★★ *Complicated* — *Fairly expensive*

EMBROIDERED DESIGNS

ACCESSORIES AND DECORATIVE EFFECTS

Introduction

Beads can be used in so many different ways. Discover a multitude of designs in this book to suit all sorts of tastes. A beaded flower for your hair or to brighten up the handle of a handbag; a decorated make-up pouch or a dazzling beaded lampshade. There are designs for the home, beautiful jewellery to keep or give as treasured gifts and some lovely ideas for adding sparkling motifs to clothes. Use these designs as inspiration and add your own personal touch to make your own unique creations.

The designs in this book have been inspired by the natural world, exotic designs, colours and contemporary trends. Easy-to-follow, step-by-step instructions introduce easy to complex techniques which allow your creative talents to expand to tackle all sorts of projects.

In '1001 beads', beads of all shapes and colours combine with a multitude of materials like ribbons, charms, tubing and sequins to make stunning party jewellery, fashion accessories and home decorations.

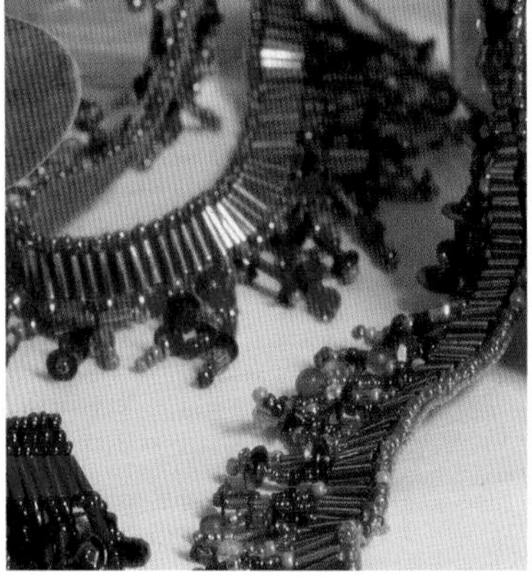

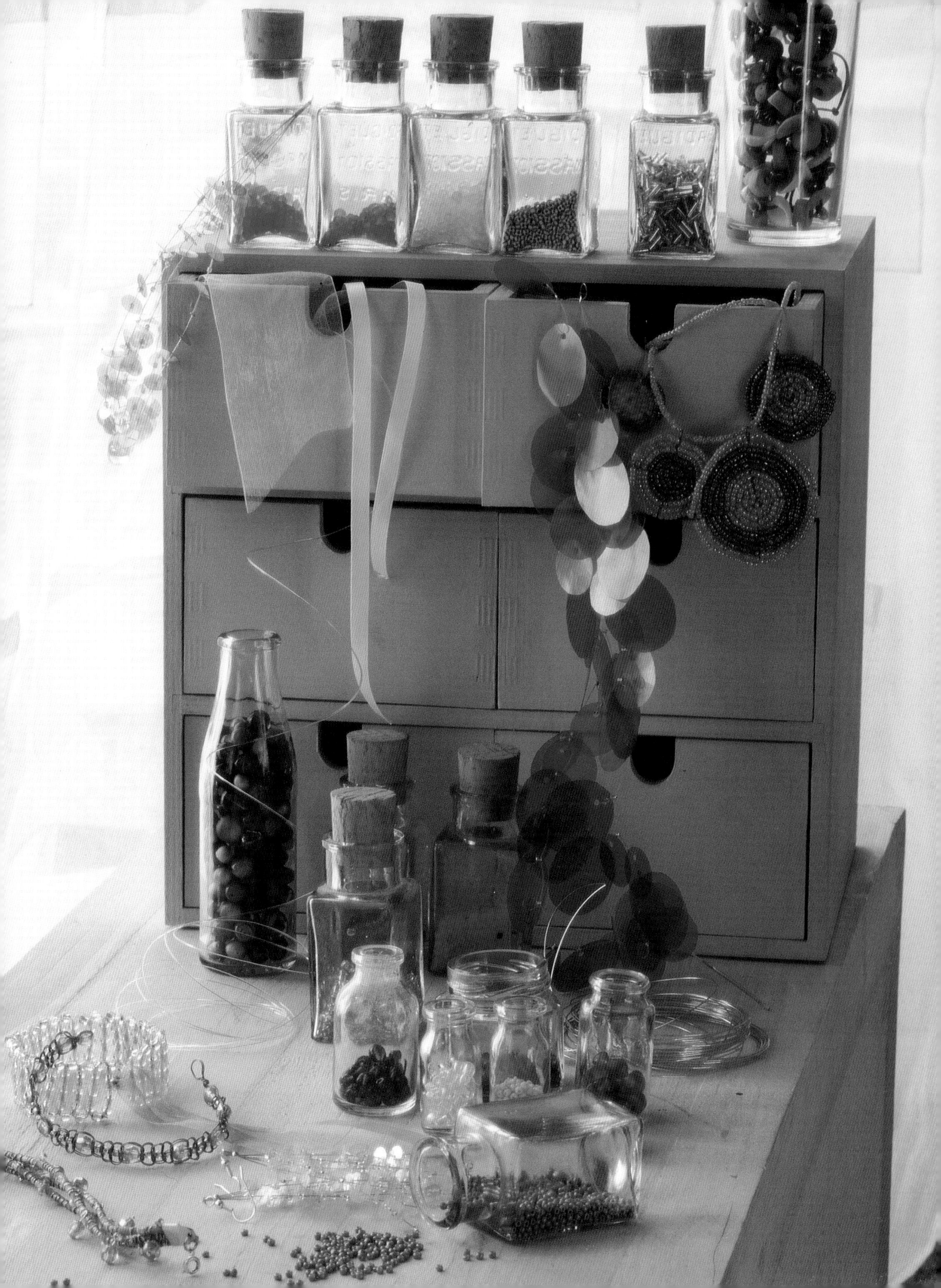

Beads and Sequins

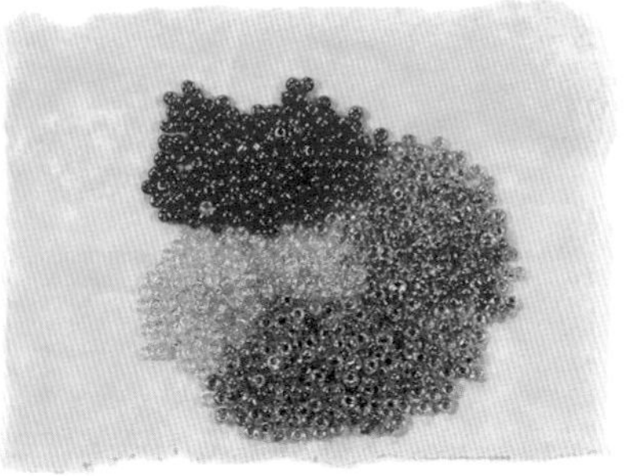

Small clear glass beads: small glass beads in a variety of colours; the smallest glass beads are used in embroidery work.

Faceted beads: in plastic or glass, these are made in many different colours and sizes. They also come in iridescent finishes.

Clay beads: you can make these at home using air-drying clay (see Rustic Clay Necklace, page 34).

Small opaque glass beads: come in gold and silver, too. Used to accentuate the outlines of designs.

Bugles (long beads): in embroidery these are used either as flower stems or laid out side by side. They can be used with other beads to make fringe designs.

Wooden beads: these can be interspersed with other beads and work especially well combined with clay beads.

Tissue paper beads: lightweight beads in a wide variety of colours that you can make at home (see Handmade Paper Beads, page 56).

Faceted sequins with centre holes: may be clear, opaque, shiny or iridescent, and come in a variety of sizes and colours.

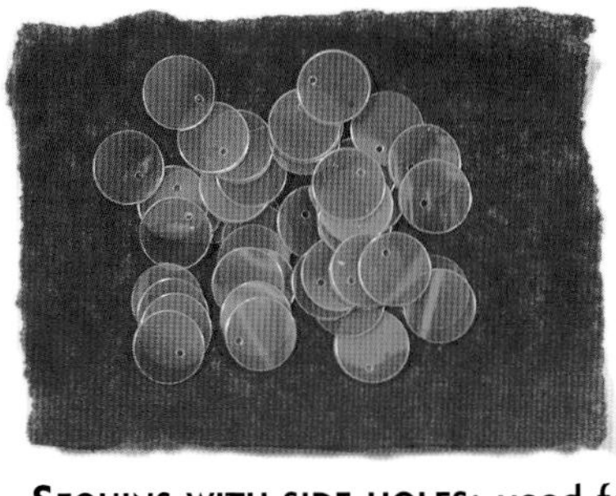

Sequins with side holes: used for making pendants and in fringe work.

Charms: can be interspersed with other beads or used as individual decorations.

Shells: pierced shells can be purchased from specialist shops or collected from beaches and pierced at home.

Crimp beads: small metal beads used for securing threads when knotting is impractical. Use them on wire and nylon thread.

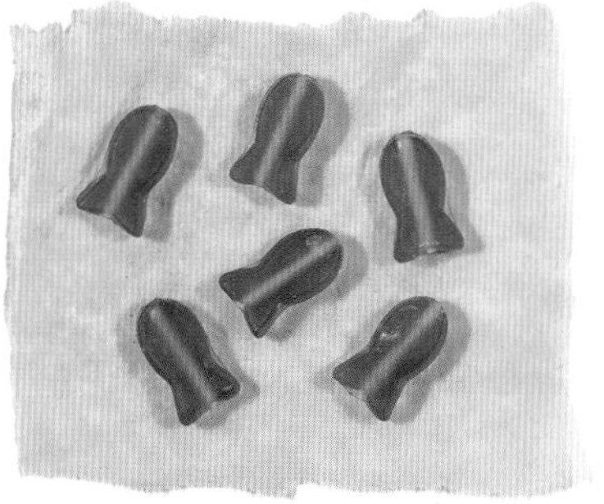

Novelty beads: come in a wide variety of colours, sizes, materials and shapes. Select them according to the object you wish to decorate.

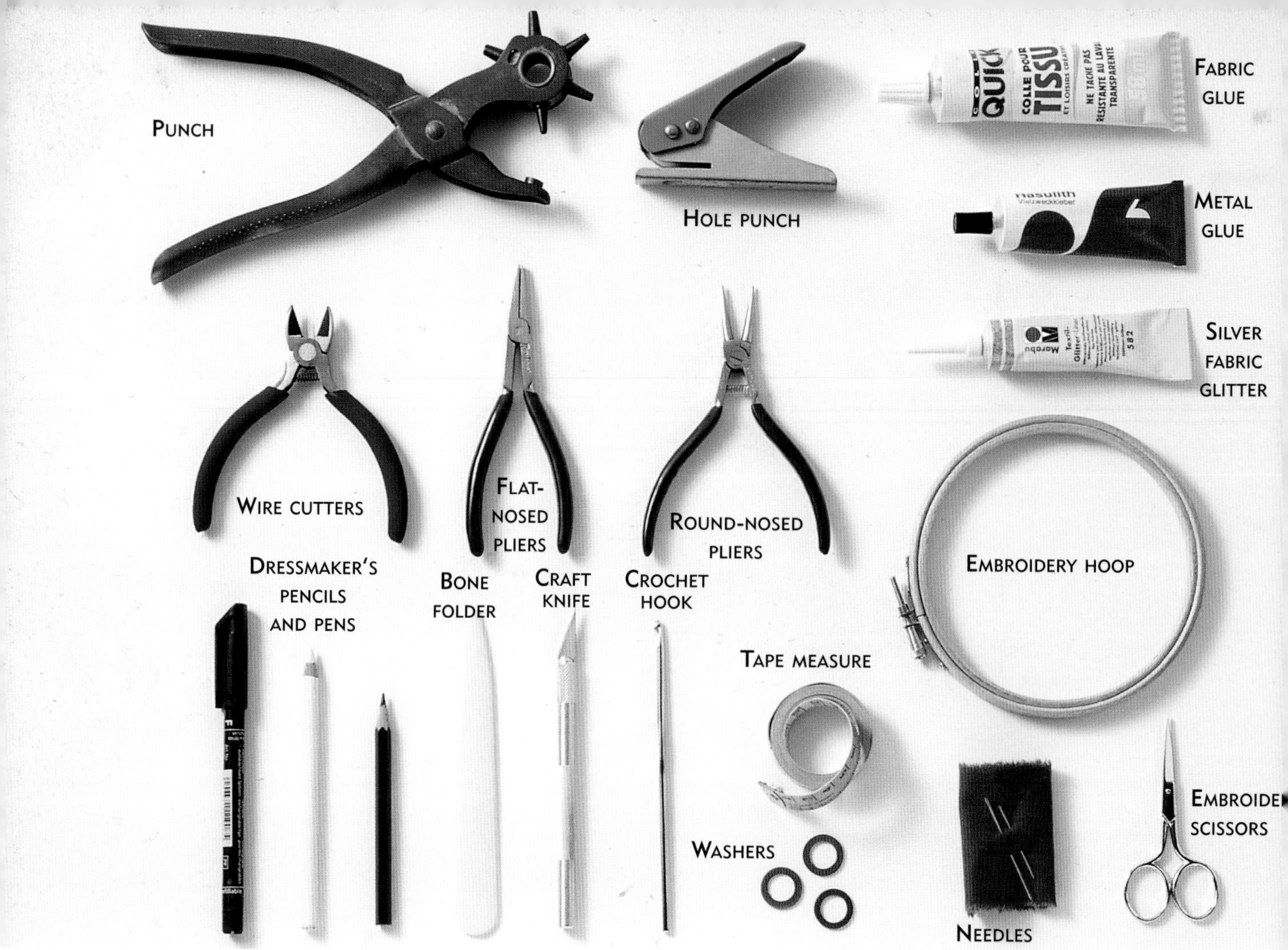
Punch
Hole punch
Fabric glue
Metal glue
Silver fabric glitter
Wire cutters
Flat-nosed pliers
Round-nosed pliers
Embroidery hoop
Dressmaker's pencils and pens
Bone folder
Craft knife
Crochet hook
Tape measure
Washers
Needles
Embroide
scissors

Basic Equipment

Silver fabric glitter: gives a sparkly effect; squeeze the tube lightly and apply directly to the fabric.

Metal glue: for gluing two pieces of metal together; leave to dry for 12 hours.

Fabric glue: a special glue that is invisible when dry.

Washers: small drilled-out discs available from hardware stores. Used for creating small mirrors (see Ethnic Make-Up Pouch, page 84).

Tools

Round-nosed and flat-nosed pliers: essential for working with and shaping wire.

Wire cutters: for cutting wire of different thicknesses.

Punch: for making holes of varying sizes in thicker materials such as suede ribbon.

Hole punch: has one hole size and is ideal for feltwork.

Embroidery hoop: an essential tool for embroidering on canvas. Place the canvas over the smaller circle, push the larger circle into position and tighten the screw to secure.

Crochet hook: comes in different sizes.

Embroidery scissors: used for precise cutting and trimming work.

Craft knife: has a sharp blade for precise cutting work.

Bone folder: made from horn or plastic, this tool is used to help bend materials.

Needles: the size of the needle is dictated by the thickness of the thread. For beadwork, use a long, fine needle.

Tape measure: for wrist and neck measurements.

Dressmaker's pencils and pens: for marking out designs on fabric.

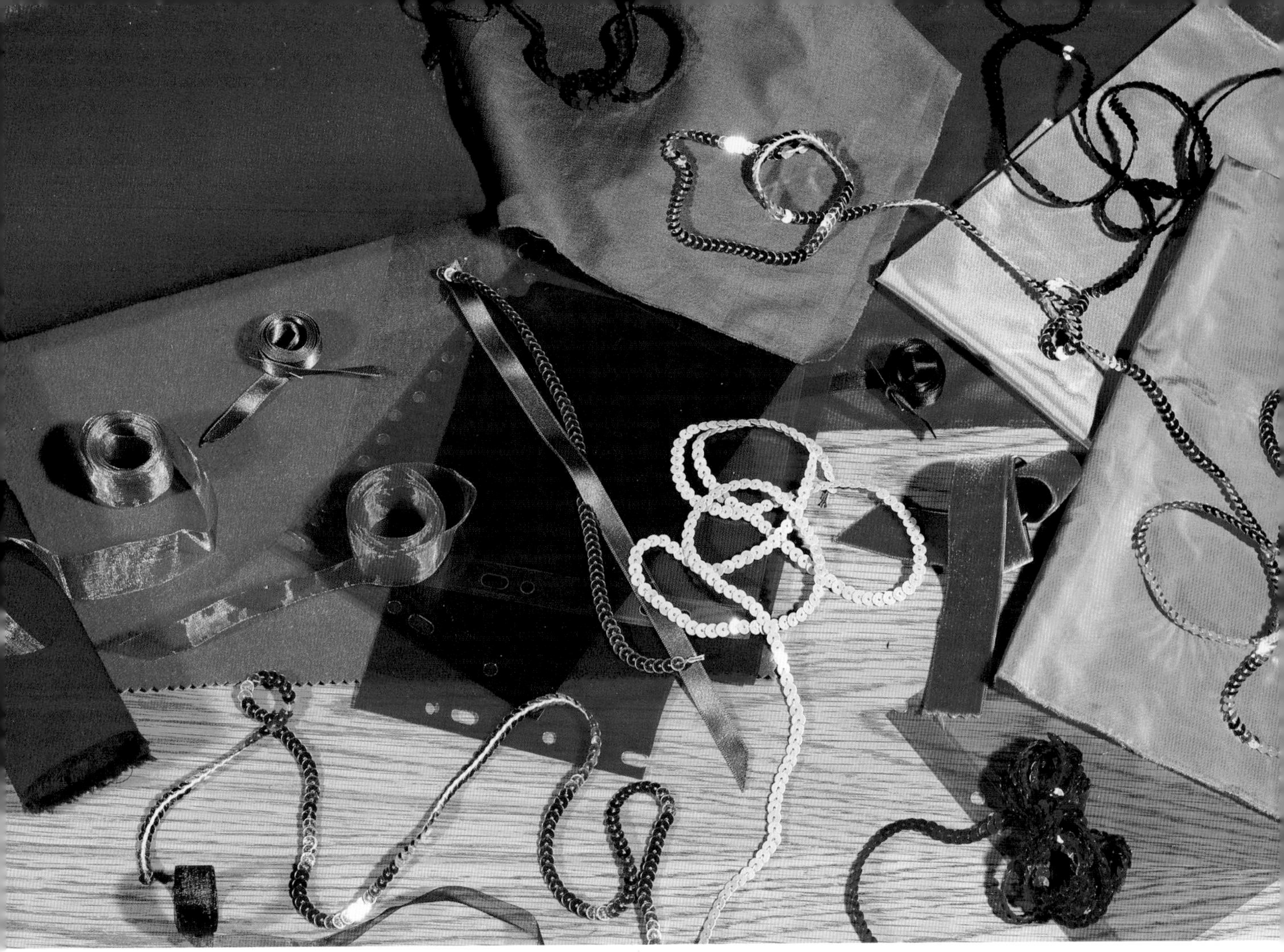

Fabric and Ribbons

Ensure that you always choose good quality fabric that will hold its shape well while you work.

Organza, satin and taffeta: come in a variety of colours, the vast majority of them shimmering. They lend pizzazz and sparkle to your creations.

Silk: used for making special pieces of jewellery and small accessories embroidered with beads.

Tarlatan: an inexpensive transparent fabric which comes in a variety of shades. With the added advantage of being easy to cut, tarlatan holds its shape well and does not fray. If you are unable to find coloured tarlatan, dye your fabric using a dampened foam roller and some coloured ink.

Canvas: you can find canvas in any haberdashery departments and fabric stores. Use fine canvas for embroidering with beads. Don't be afraid to ask for advice, as the gauge of the canvas must be appropriate for the size of the beads you are using.

Felt: felt and fleece do not fray; they are used as a backing material in designs incorporating beads.

Cotton: available in a wide range of colours, cottons are used in embroidered jewellery and accessories.

Velvet, satin and sheer ribbons: used as backing materials for embroidering beads.

Grosgrain: grosgrain ribbons are fairly stiff and are ideal for jewellery work.

Plastic sheets: come in a wide variety of colours and can be cut easily with scissors. Used for making sequins.

Stitched sequins: these sequins are sold by the metre and come pre-stitched together. They can be purchased in a wide variety of colours.

Flat ends

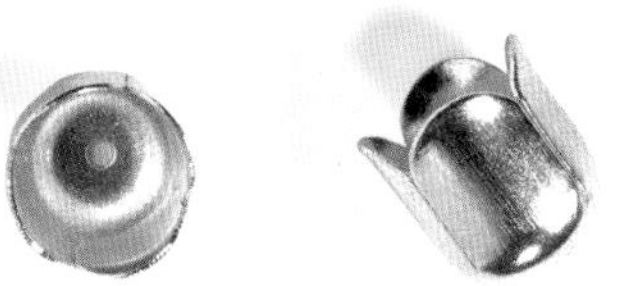
End caps

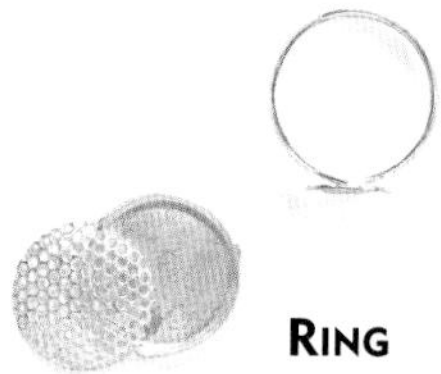
Ring mountings

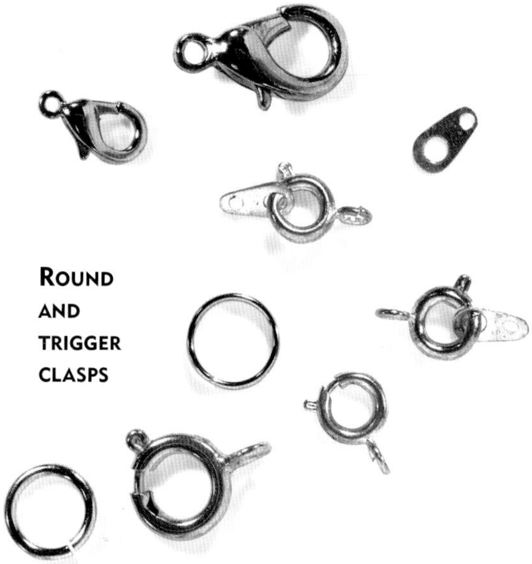
Round and trigger clasps

Clasps and Mounts

Flat ends: used for finishing ribbon jewellery they have a hole to attach the clasp.

End caps: for finishing items of jewellery that have several wires or threads or a very thick wire.

Round and trigger clasps: suitable for use on all types of jewellery and widely available.

Jump rings: linked to clasps to offer greater freedom of movement.

Cylindrical clasp for metal necklaces: does not require a link ring. Simply place the wire into the clasp and secure with pliers.

Multirow clasp: for making up jewellery with multiple rows.

Eye pins: used for making pendants and clasp rings.

Press-studs: fastenings for jewellery made from fabric and ribbon.

Safety pin: used to attach items of jewellery to clothing or accessories.

Mounts and findings: for creating rings, brooches, hairclips and earrings.

Jump rings

Press-studs

Safety pin

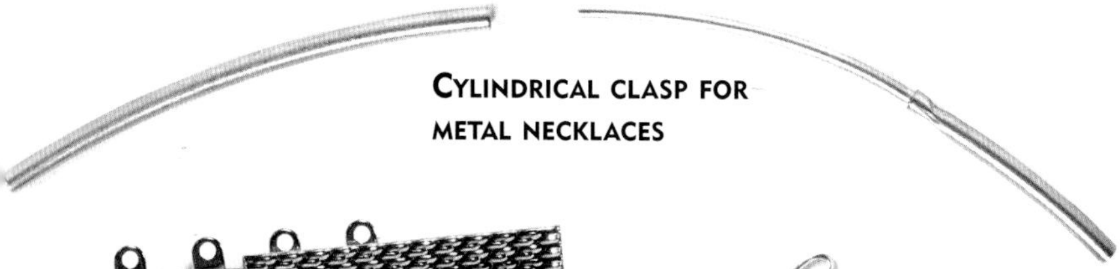
Cylindrical clasp for metal necklaces

Brooch mounts

Multirow clasp

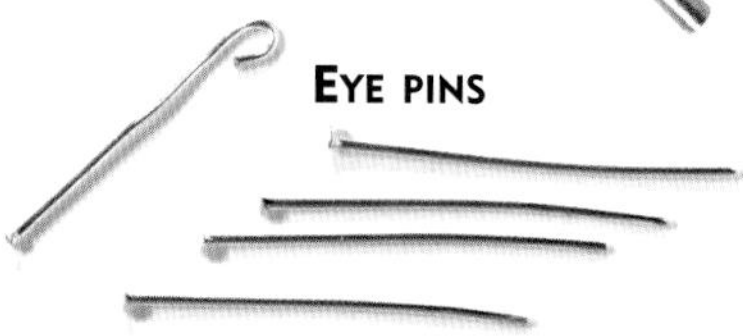
Eye pins

Hairclip mounts

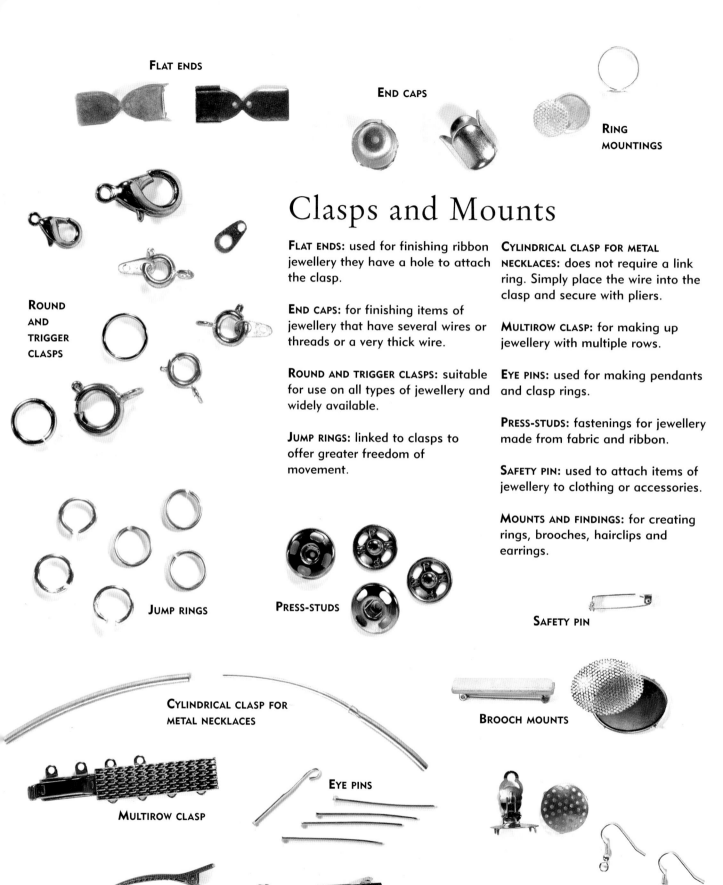

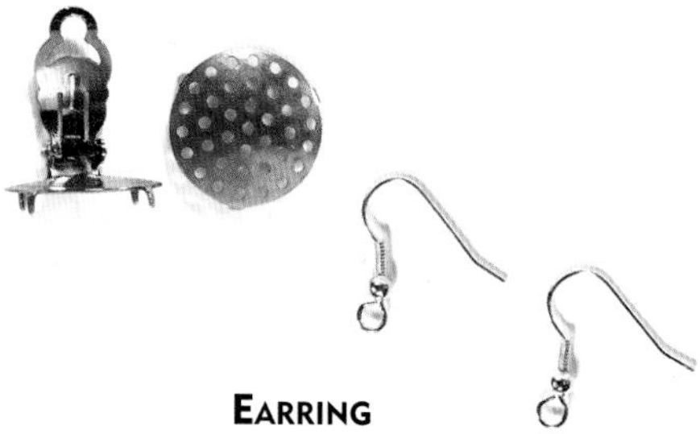
Earring findings

Plastic tubing

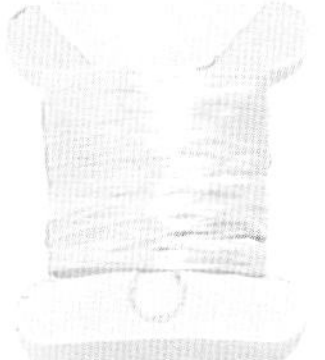

Elasticated nylon thread

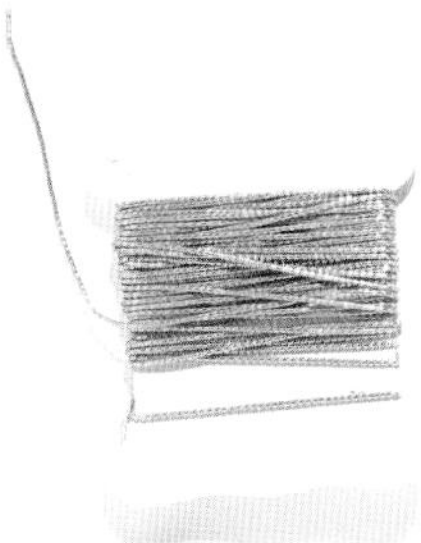

Elasticated gold thread

Wire

Threads and Wires

Elasticated nylon thread: thinner than standard elastic, this thread is easier to pass through small beads.

Elasticated gold thread: ideal for threading on large beads and can be used without a clasp.

Coloured wire: a strong wire that does not kink. Used for creating necklaces and bracelets.

Coloured enamelled wire 0.3mm (1/64in) diameter: easy to work with, this wire remains visible in places and forms part of the overall decorative effect.

Thin wire 0.3mm (1/64in) diameter: comes in a variety of colours and is ideal for delicate work.

Wire 0.8mm (1/32in) diameter: this thicker wire is used as a base for certain types of beaded jewellery.

Plastic tubing: can be cut into small pieces and used as beads; comes in a variety of bright colours.

Rat-tail cord: this 3mm (1/8in) diameter cord has a shiny and silky appearance and comes in a wide variety of colours.

Embroidery threads/silks: made up of six strands that can be separated.

Leather thonging: comes in several colours; used with beads with large holes and in designs where the thread is visible.

Rubber tubing: comes in a range of diameters; strings of beads can be wrapped around the tubing to create unique designs.

Thin wire

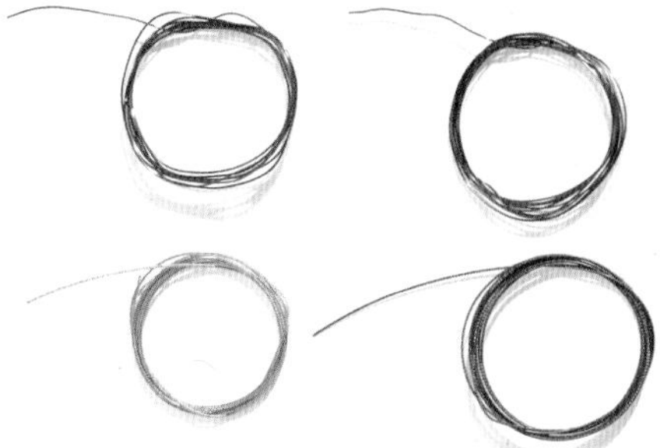

Coloured enamelled wire

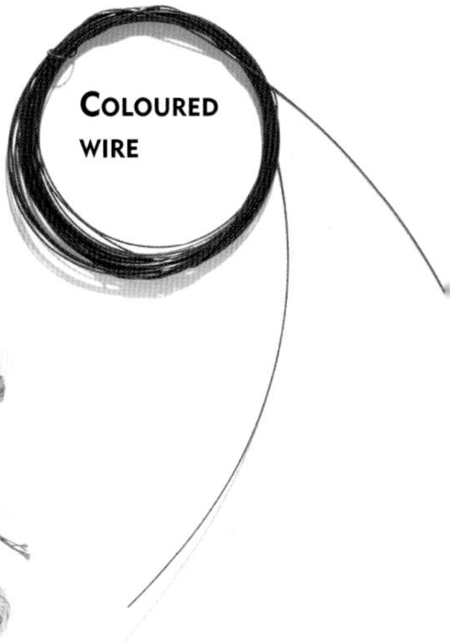

Coloured wire

Rubber tubing

Leather thonging

Rat-tail cord

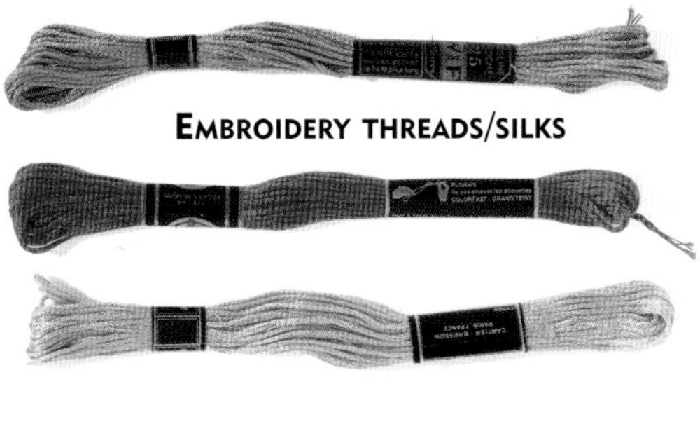

Embroidery threads/silks

Chain Stitch

This is the most important of the looped stitches, a family of stitches that includes blanket stitch (see page 15) and feather stitch (see page 16). It is also one of the most widely employed stitches in embroidery. Used all over the world, it is said to be of Indian or Persian origin, where craftspeople use a small crochet hook called an *ari* in their stitching. It is widely used in ethnic embroidery.

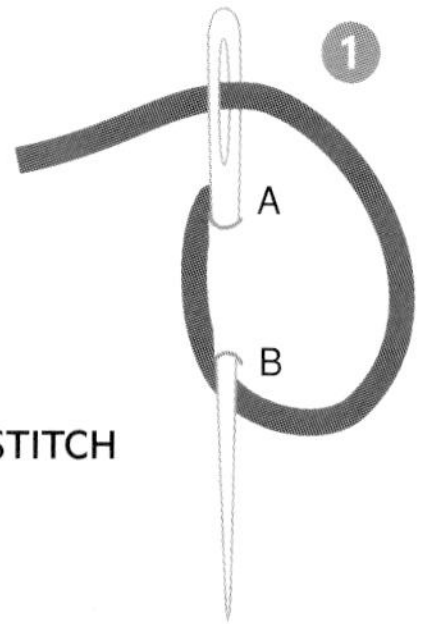
1
A
B

CHAIN STITCH

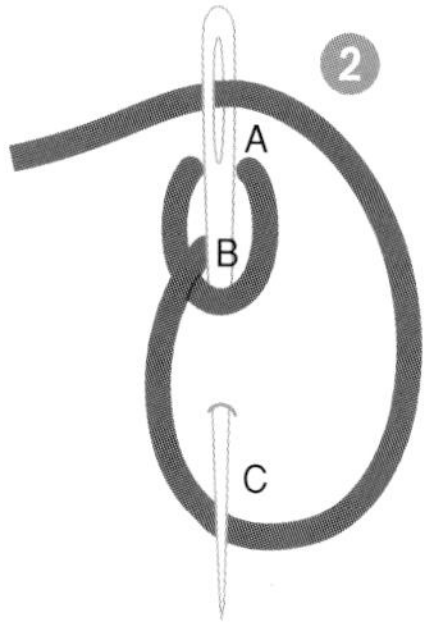
2
A
B
C

3

LAZY DAISY STITCH

1 Bring the needle up at A, then insert back into A and bring out at B. Carry the thread under the point of the needle.

2 Pull the thread through and insert the needle back into B. Bring out at C, carrying the thread under the point of the needle.

3 Sew a detached chain stitch by repeating step 1. Pull the thread through and sew a small stitch to hold the loop in place. Stitch five loops in a circle to create a flower.

TECHNICAL TIPS

Different results can be achieved depending on the type of thread and fabric that you use. Experiment with the stitch by working on thick fabric and leftover pieces of fine silk using one or more strands of embroidery thread and alter the technique used as you work.

As this is a relief stitch, you should keep it fairly loose, and try to keep the stitches the same size without pulling on the thread too much.

Chain stitch is suited to different thicknesses of thread, from individual strands to thick embroidery threads. The stitch is also well suited to fabrics with an uneven weave. Choose the thread, needle and stitch size to suit the surface to be embroidered.

To make a zigzag chain stitch insert your needle on the diagonal, first to the left, then to the right of the central line of your motif.

Detached chain stitch

Individual chain stitches are secured with a small stitch. Used for stitching motifs and for filling in areas, they are very versatile. When used as an infilling stitch, they are usually worked in rows or concentric circles.

USES AND VARIATIONS

- Chain stitch is used principally for borders and infilling. When worked to fill in an area the rows are stitched closely together, using one colour, threads in contrasting colours or colours that shade off gradually. In this way you can achieve different results every time.
- Chain stitch variations are widely used in contemporary embroidery.
- Detached chain stitch is worked in the same way as standard chain stitch, but each stitch is isolated and secured with a small stitch.
- Stitching around in a circle creates a flower shape, which is known as lazy daisy stitch (see diagram 3, above).

Buttonhole and Blanket Stitches

These two stitches belong to the family of looped stitches. The technique used for each one is the same; the only difference lies in the spacing between each stitch. Buttonhole stitches are worked close together, blanket stitches are spaced at regular intervals. The names of the two stitches are often used interchangeably in embroidery books.

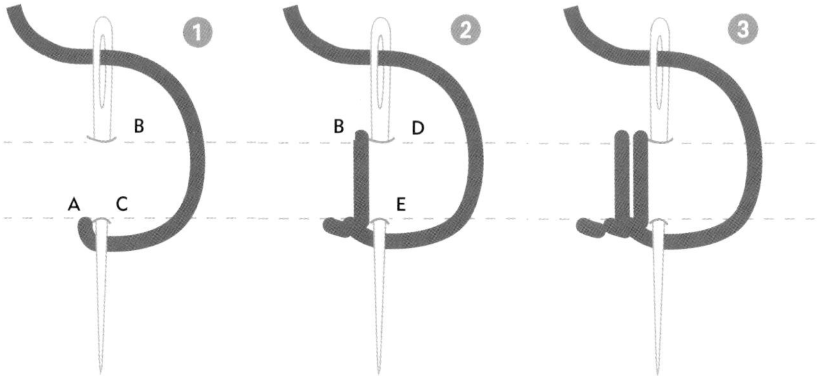

1
B
A C
2
B D
E
3

1 Bring the needle up at A, then in again at B. Come up at C, level with A. Pull the thread through, carrying it under the point of the needle.

2 Insert the needle at D, level with B. Come up at E, carrying the thread under the point of the needle.

3 Repeat this pattern as you work along the row, keeping the stitches even and carrying the thread under the point of the needle.

Basic equipment and materials
You should ensure above all that the material you choose is appropriate for what you intend to use it for: a cushion cover, for example, will require a hard-wearing and preferably washable fabric. Check also that needle and thread will pass through the fabric without splitting the material threads. Lastly, you will find a pair of small sharp scissors invaluable for cutting motifs and designs.

Technical tips

The main difficulty with this stitch is keeping the stitch height even. It may help to draw out two faint guidelines on the material using a dressmaker's pencil. Work from left to right, ensuring that the stitches are kept taut but not so taut that the fabric gathers. The stitches should be evenly spaced; ensure that they are as close as possible to one another for buttonhole stitch or that you maintain the same distance between each one for blanket stitch.

Uses and variations

- Buttonhole stitch was originally used for stitching along straight or rounded edges, because it made the edges stronger and was aesthetically appealing. It is widely used in embroidery, especially with openwork motifs. It is a classic of traditional and contemporary embroidery. This is a great filler stitch which not only lends depth and relief to motifs but also allows you to create flower motifs and pyramid and ladder effects.
- The most basic variation involves varying the stitch height by working alternate short and long stitches. For best results, ensure that you always keep the base row even and the stitch heights constant.
- The stitch can also be worked on the diagonal or radiating outwards from a central circle.

Feather Stitch

Feather stitch is another member of the looped stitch family. The stitch is very popular and highly decorative and is widely known throughout the Anglo-Saxon world as a means of creating smocking and crazy patchwork.

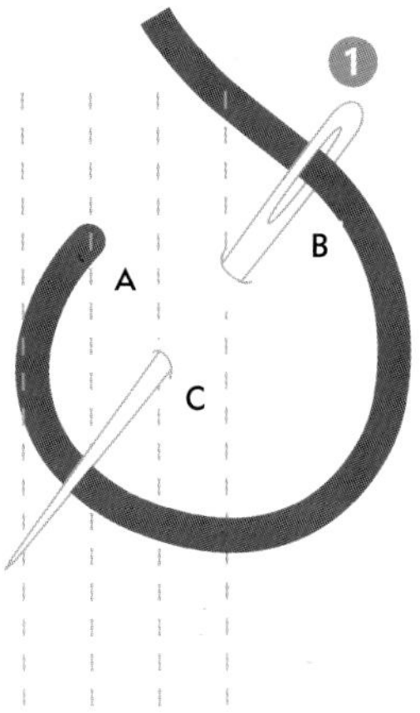
1
A
B
C

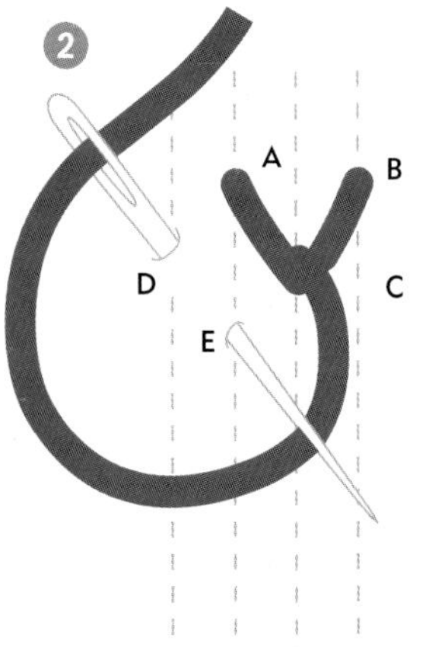
2
A
B
D
C
E

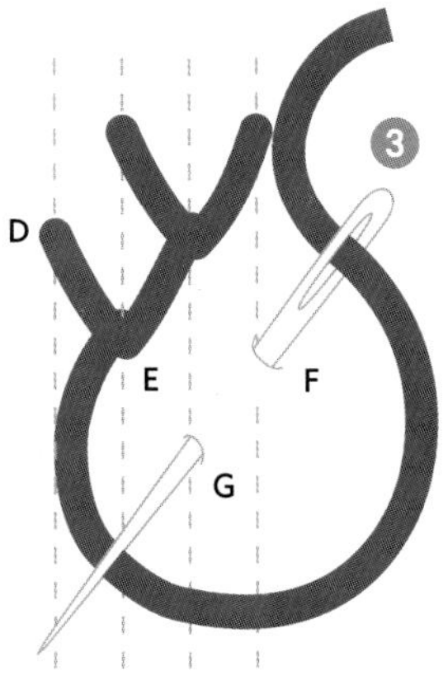
3
D
E
F
G

Feather stitch is worked from top to bottom.

1 Bring the needle out at A, then into B, on the same level as A. Come out again at C, carrying the thread under the point of the needle.

2 Pull the thread through and go into D, on the same level as C. Come out at E, carrying the thread under the point of the needle.

3 Continue working in this way. Go into F, on the same level as E and come out at G, carrying the thread under the point of the needle.

Technical tips

Feather stitch is easier to work than it appears, but achieving truly satisfying results may take some time and patience. Start by working between vertical rows. Draw four evenly spread vertical lines on the fabric to help keep the stitches even. Ensure that you always insert the needle into the fabric towards the centre from top to bottom. Once you have become more proficient you can start to experiment with more complex patterns.
This stitch is suitable for use on any type of fabric, but when you are starting out you will find it easier to work on fabrics with a visible weave.
Select the needles and threads according to the thickness and texture of the material you are working on.

Uses and variations

- Feather stitch is often used in traditional embroidery for filling in leaf designs because its delicate alternating motif looks a little like leaf veining. Feather stitch is also used for stunning border work on straight or curved edges, and is often worked in contrasting colours. You can create fine and delicate motifs such as branches using a single strand of embroidery thread. This stitch can be used for sewing pieces of fabric together and for concealing seams. It is also used for decorating selvages and hems.
- The stitch has many variations, including double, triple and quadruple feather stitch, involving two, three or four stitches worked consecutively to the left and then to the right in a zigzag pattern.

Covering large areas
Resist the temptation to use very long lengths of thread: if threads over 45cm (18in) in length are used they will tangle, fray and lose their shine.

French Seam

1. Place two pieces of fabric wrong sides together. Sew a seam 0.6cm (1/4in) from the edge.
2. Fold the fabric back right sides together, flatten out the seam and sew another seam 0.6cm (1/4in) from the edge, enclosing the first seam that you made.
3. Turn the fabric out and iron. The result is a clean seam which does not require further stitching.

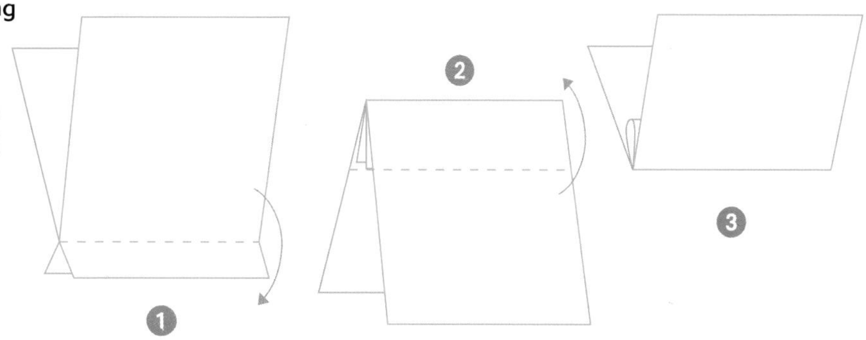

1
2
3

Running Stitch

The most basic of all stitches. Used for joining two pieces of fabric together or as a simple outline or decorative stitch. It is important to keep the lengths of the stitches uniform.

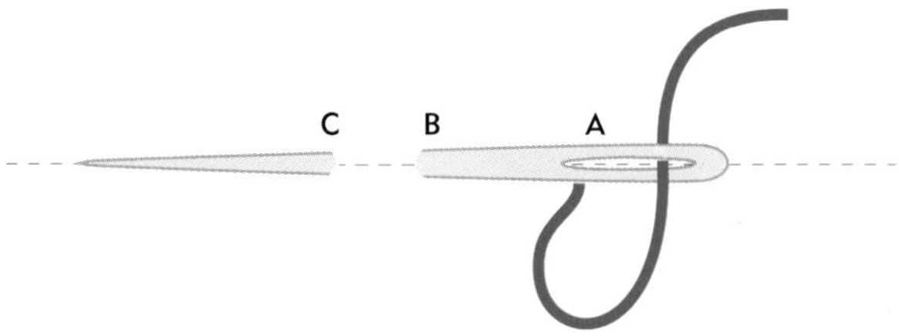

C
B
A

Bring the needle up at A, down at B, then up again at C. Pull the thread through and begin the sequence again.

Ladder Stitch

This is used principally for stitching together two pieces of fabric with concealed stitching.

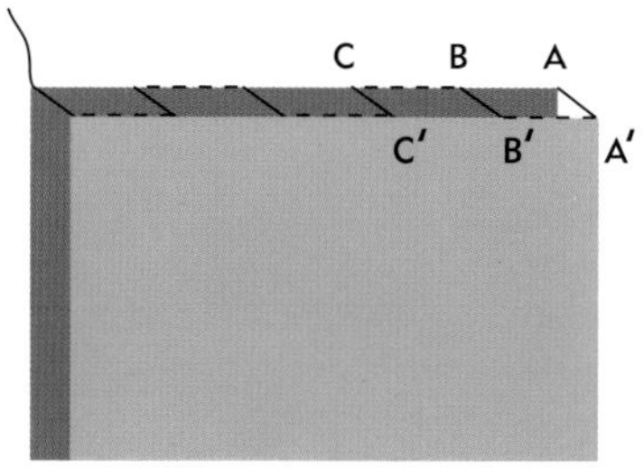

C
B
A
C′
B′
A′

Insert the needle at A, then into A′. Pass the needle under the fold in the front piece of fabric and come out at B then in again at B′. Repeat this pattern until the row is completed.

Springy Bead Bracelets ★★

Materials required

- *2 large beads*
- *sprung bracelet or choker wire*
- *1m (39in) thin, coloured enamelled copper or metal wire*
- *small glass beads*

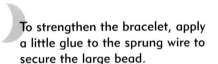

To strengthen the bracelet, apply a little glue to the sprung wire to secure the large bead.

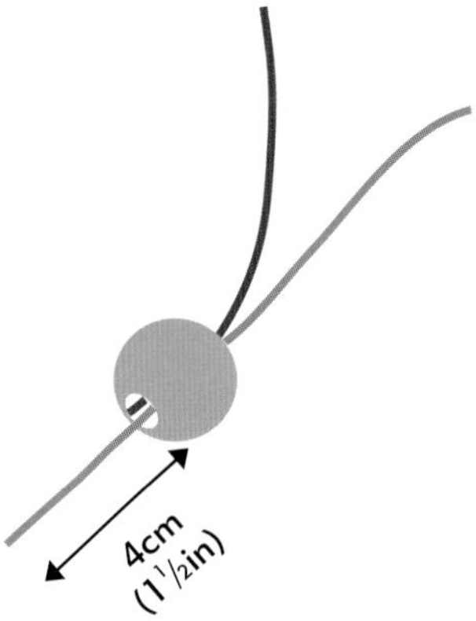
4cm
(1½in)

1 Thread one of the large beads on one end of the sprung wire. Thread 4cm (1½in) of the thin wire through the same bead.

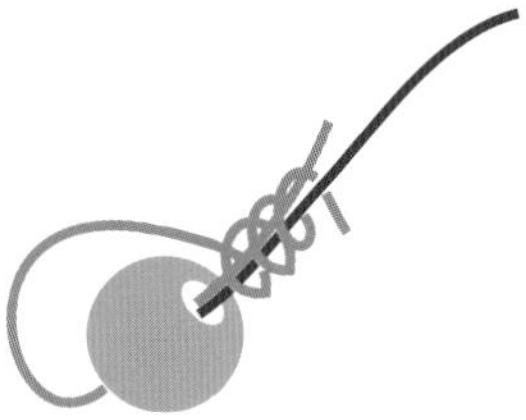

2 Keeping the large bead at the end of the sprung wire, bend the 4cm (1½in) length of thin wire back over the top of the large bead and wind it tightly around both wires to secure.

Sprung wire is bent into shape and does not require a clasp fastening.

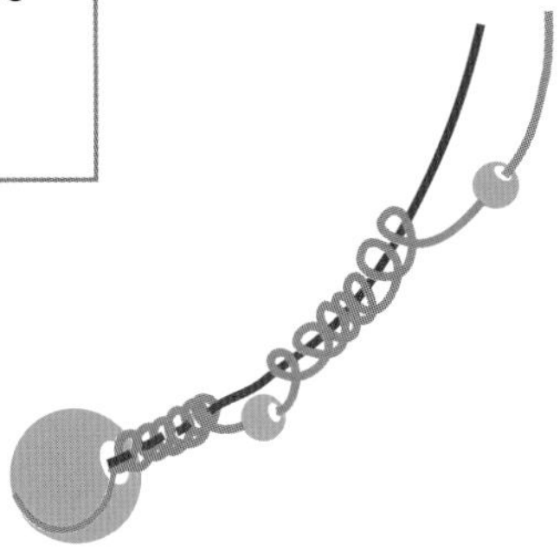

3 Thread a small glass bead on to the remaining length of thin wire and wrap it roughly six times around the sprung wire, before adding another small glass bead. Continue until the sprung wire is covered.

4 Finish the bracelet in the same way that you started it: thread the remaining large bead on to the sprung and thin wire and bend the wire back over the top of the large bead. Wind it tightly around the sprung bracelet to secure.

Bead Cascades ★★

Materials required

ORANGE, RED AND MAUVE NECKLACE

- *5 x 1m (39in) lengths of silver wire*
- *4-ringed clasp in silver*
- *8 crimp beads*
- *flat-nosed pliers*
- *jewellery glue*
- *large faceted beads in mauve and purple*
- *faceted beads in deep red, mauve and orange*
- *small glass beads in orange and red*
- *clear sequins in orange*
- *wire cutters*

Ensure that you select large enough beads for the ends of the necklace: they should be able to hold four wires. It is important to encase wire ends inside beads as they can irritate the skin.

This is a stunning necklace that is very simple to make. For a party piece, make two or three and wear them together.

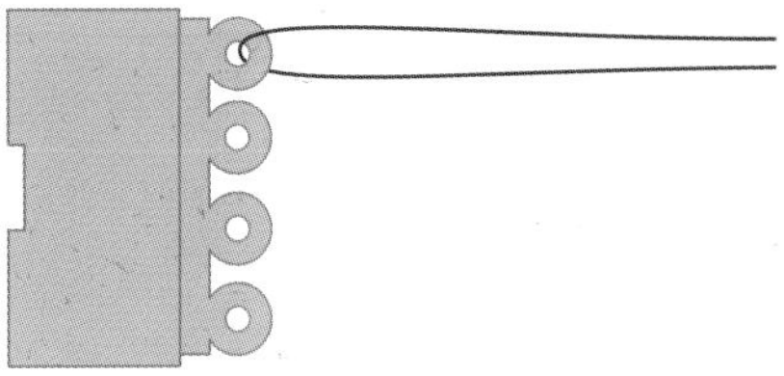

1 Thread a length of silver wire through the first ring on one half of the clasp. Bring the two ends together to make two equal lengths.

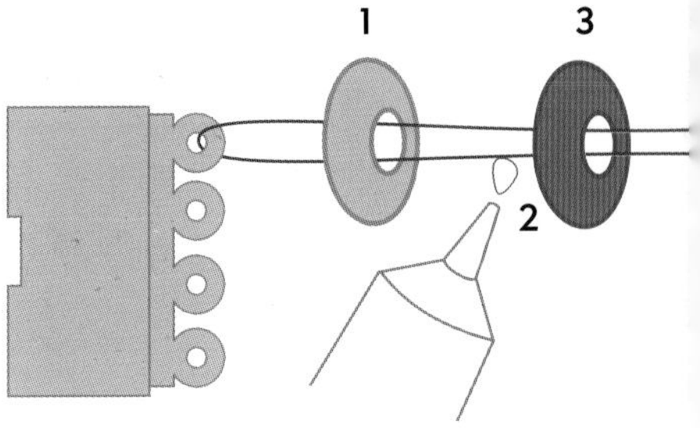
1
3
2

2 Thread both wires through a crimp bead. Use the flat-nosed pliers to squeeze the crimp 3mm (1/8in) from the clasp. Apply a dab of glue to the wire just beside the crimp bead then thread on a large purple bead and position it over the glue.

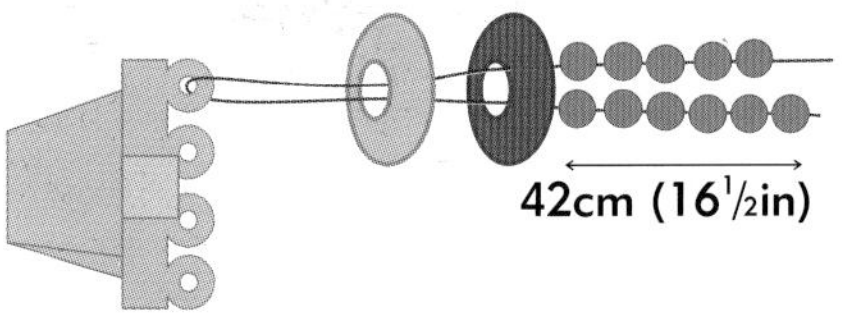
42cm (16½in)

3 Next, thread on two rows of beads over 42cm (16½in), breaking up the small glass beads with large and small faceted beads and sequins and varying the colours as you go. Use the photograph opposite for inspiration or create your own designs.

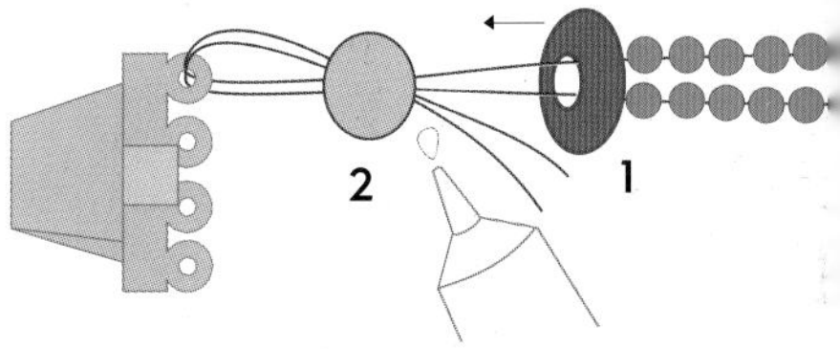
2
1

4 To finish off, thread the two wires through a large purple bead and then a crimp. Thread the two wires through the first ring of the other half of the clasp and take them back through the crimp bead. Squeeze the crimp using flat-nosed pliers 3mm (1/8in) from the clasp.

5 Cut the excess wire 1.5mm (1/16in) from the crimp bead. Glue the large purple bead to the wire and thread the ends of the wire into the centre of the bead. Repeat the same process for all four rings of the clasp.

Constellations

Materials required

BLUE NECKLACE

- *4 x 50cm (20in) lengths of silver wire*
- *strong metal glue*
- *small glass beads in pale blue*
- *clear coloured sequins in pale blue*
- *cylindrical necklace clasp in silver*
- *flat-nosed pliers*

There is no need to wait for the small glass beads to dry on the wire as the strong glue should take immediate effect.

For a more complex design, you could alternate the colours and shapes of the sequins on each of the wires.

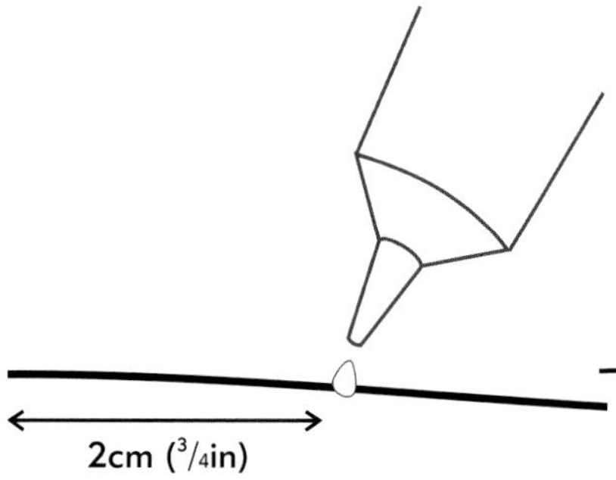
2cm ($^{3}/_{4}$in)

❶ Put a dab of glue 2cm ($^{3}/_{4}$in) from one of the ends of a length of silver wire. Thread on a blue small glass bead and position it over the glue.

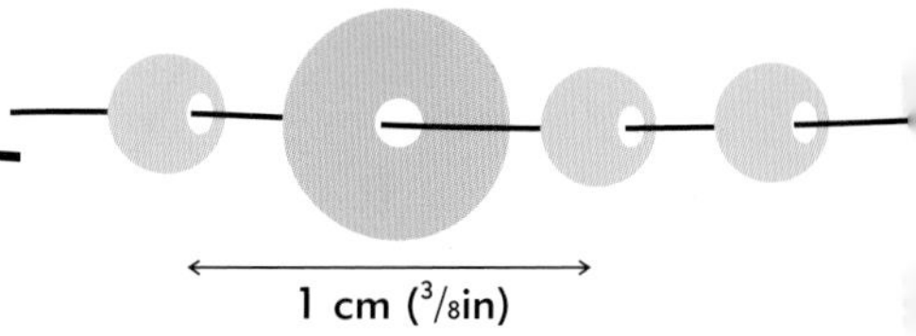
1 cm ($^{3}/_{8}$in)

❷ Next, thread on a pale blue sequin without gluing it down, then thread on another small glass bead and secure it with a dab of glue. Continue in this way, alternating between beads which are glued down and sequins which are not, leaving roughly 1cm ($^{3}/_{8}$in) between the small glass beads. Finish with a bead 2cm ($^{3}/_{4}$in) from the end of the wire. Repeat the process for the three other lengths of wires.

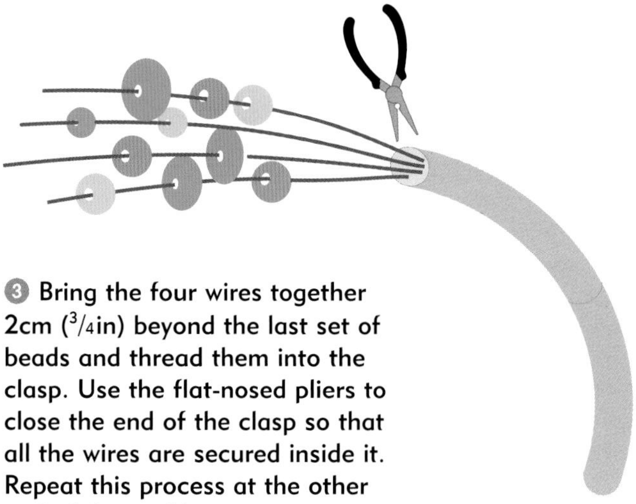

❸ Bring the four wires together 2cm ($^{3}/_{4}$in) beyond the last set of beads and thread them into the clasp. Use the flat-nosed pliers to close the end of the clasp so that all the wires are secured inside it. Repeat this process at the other end of the necklace.

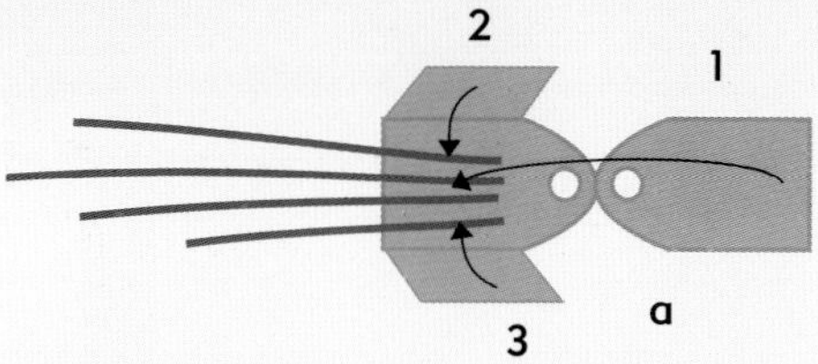
2
1
3
a

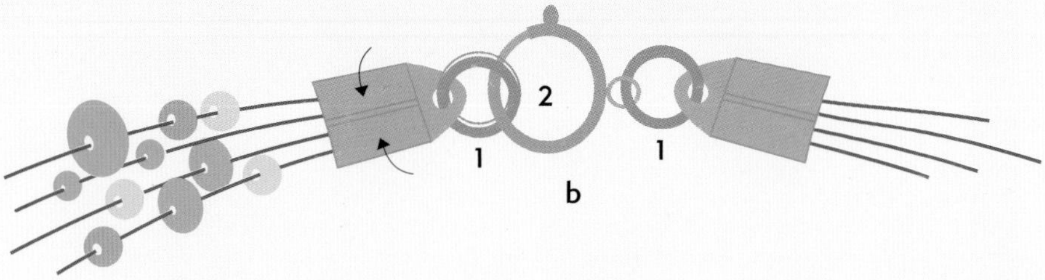
2
1
1
b

Materials required

BRACELET

- *small glass beads in pale blue*
- *clear coloured sequins in pale blue*
- *4 x 22cm ($8^3/_4$in) lengths of silver wire*
- *strong metal glue*
- *2 flat ends*
- *2 silver jump rings*
- *flat-nosed pliers*
- *silver two-holed clasp*

1 Thread the beads and sequins on to the lengths of wire (see page 22, steps 1 and 2).

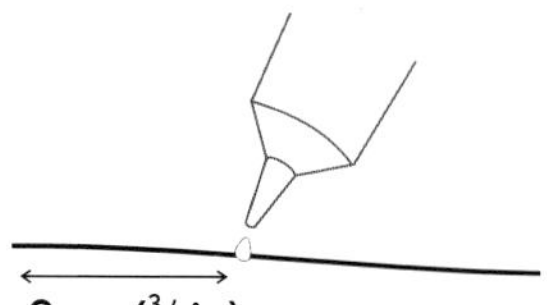
2cm ($^3/_4$in)

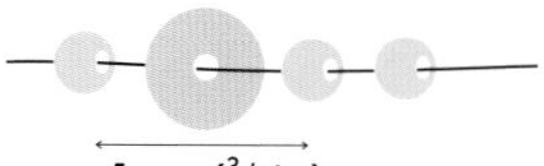
1cm ($^3/_8$in)

2 **To assemble the clasp:**
Diagram a: immediately after the last beads, place the ends of the four wires into one of the two flat ends and close the flaps down over the wires, squeezing them with the flat-nosed pliers so that they are well secured. Repeat the process at the other end of the bracelet.
Diagram b: using the flat-nosed pliers, insert a jump ring into the holes of each of the flat ends (1). Insert the clasp (2) into the rings and close the ring using the pliers.

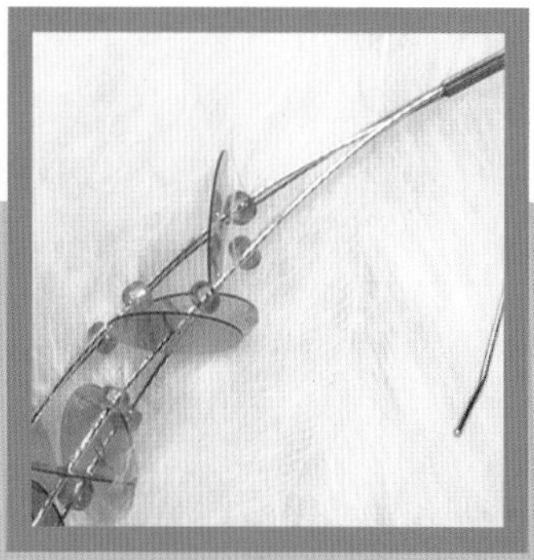

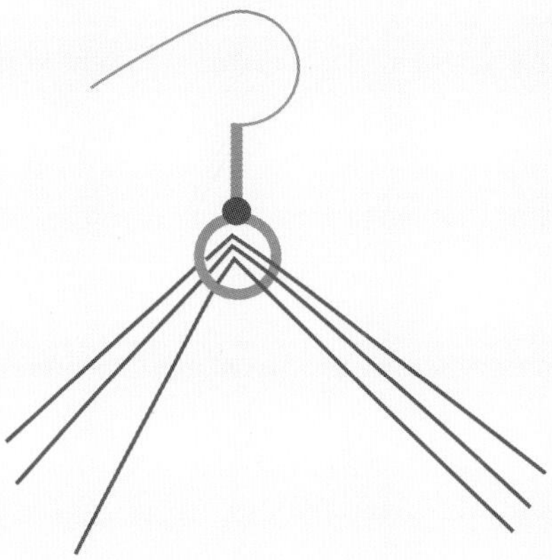

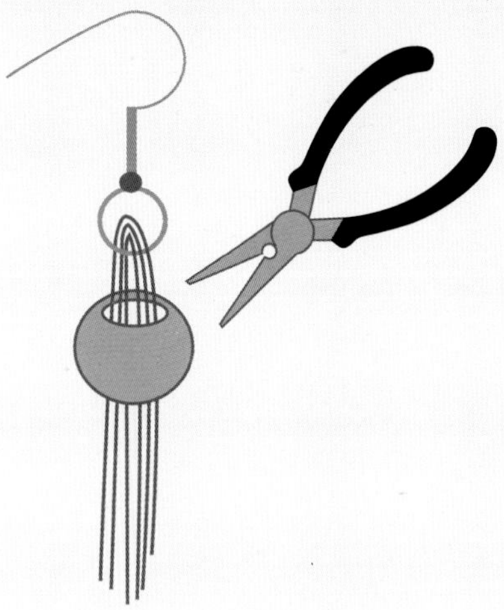

❶ Thread three lengths of wire through the hole of one of your earring findings. Bend the wire to make six equal lengths.

❷ Thread the six wires through a large crimp bead and push it up to the finding. Secure the wires by squeezing the crimp with the flat-nosed pliers.

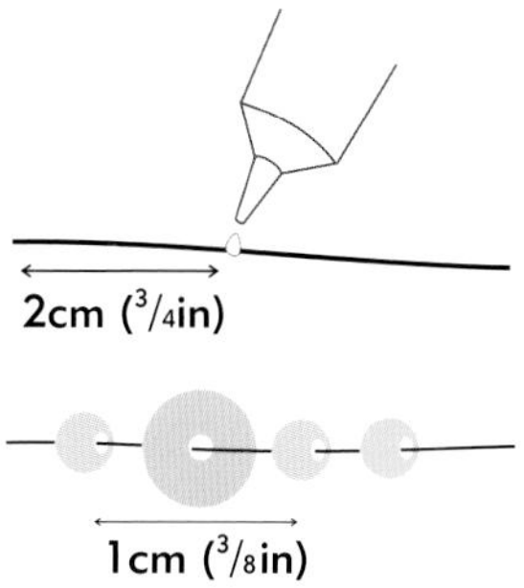
2cm (3/4in)
1cm (3/8in)

❸ Using the same technique as for the necklace and bracelet (see page 22, steps 1 and 2) thread beads and sequins on to the wires.

Materials required

EARRINGS

- *6 x 17cm (6 3/4in) lengths of silver wire*
- *2 x earring findings*
- *2 large crimp beads*
- *flat-nosed pliers*
- *clear iridescent sequins*
- *small clear glass beads in silver*
- *strong metal glue*

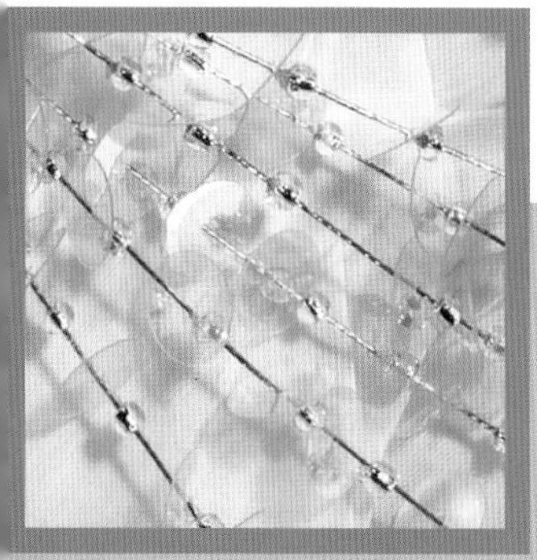

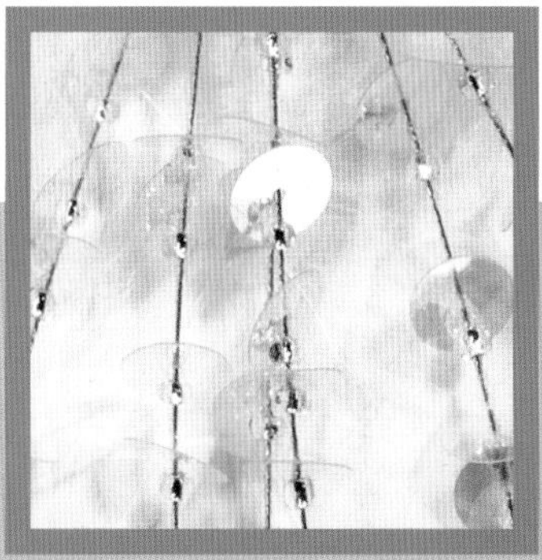

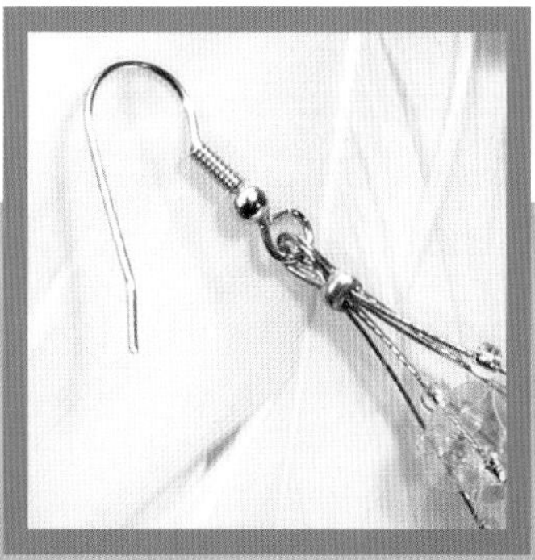

Charm Bracelets

Materials required

ORANGE BRACELET

- *20 faceted beads in orange*
- *20 metal eye pins*
- *wire cutters*
- *round-nosed pliers*
- *a fine needle*
- *30cm (12in) embroidery thread in gold*
- *3 x 22cm ($8^{3}/_{4}$in) lengths of rat-tail cord in orange*
- *15–20 small round beads in iridescent pink*
- *2 gold flat ends*
- *flat-nosed pliers*
- *2 gold jump rings*
- *gold two-holed clasp*

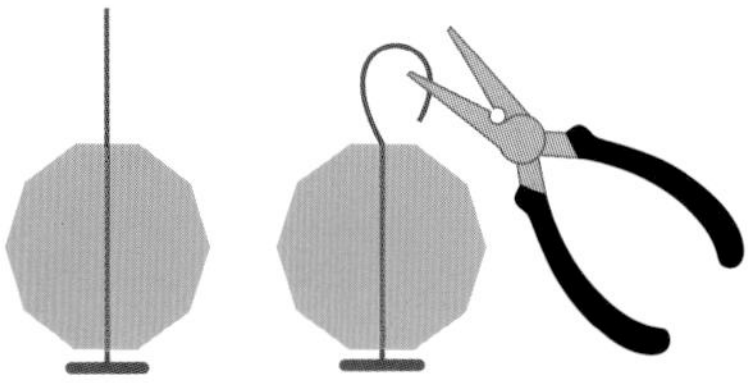

1 Start by making up twenty small pendants using the faceted beads and metal eye pins: cut the eye pins with the wire cutters 1.5cm ($^{5}/_{8}$in) from the heads. Thread on a bead and make a loop with the eye pin using the round-nosed pliers.

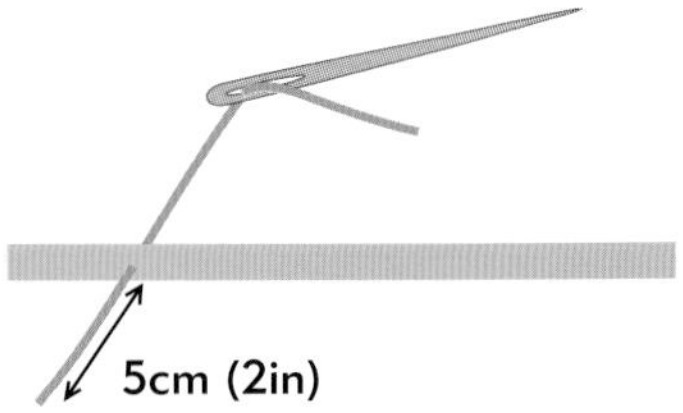
5cm (2in)

2 Thread the needle with a single strand of the gold embroidery thread. Do not knot the end of the thread. Take the needle through one end of a length of rat-tail cord, and pull the thread through leaving 5cm (2in) gold thread hanging.

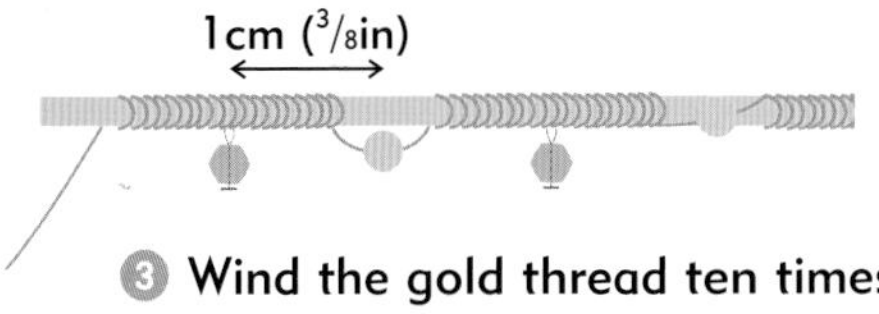
1cm ($^{3}/_{8}$in)

3 Wind the gold thread ten times around the cord: space the loops in a fairly irregular manner. Take the needle through the cord, thread on a pendant then take the needle back through the cord. Repeat this process, alternating between pendants and beads and leaving 1–2cm ($^{3}/_{8}$–$^{3}/_{4}$in) between beads and pendants. Finish by making 10 loops of gold thread at the end of the cord and taking the needle back through the cord. Decorate the two other lengths of cord in the same way.

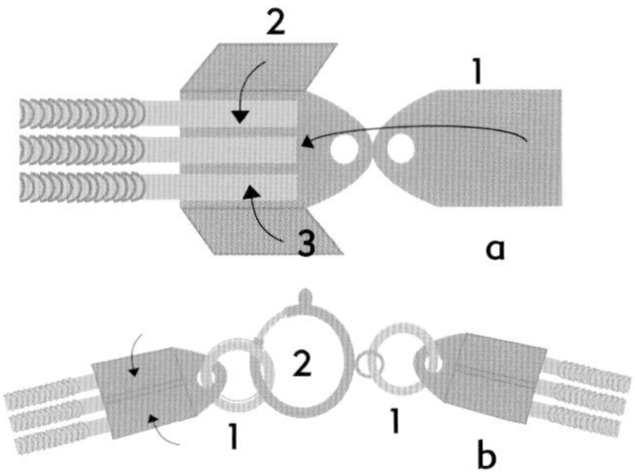
2
1
3
a
2
1
1
b

4 Trim the cords at each end to fit your wrist, then attach the clasps.
Diagram a: place the three ends of cord flat on one of the flat ends. Bend the upper part of the end down over the cords (1), then fold the two side wings down (2 and 3) and secure with the flat-nosed pliers.
Diagram b: using the flat-nosed pliers, place a jump ring in the hole of each flat end (1). Insert the clasp in the rings (2), and close with the pliers.

If the wire becomes twisted, untangle it by letting it hang loose: it will unravel itself.

Sparkling Macramé ★★★

Materials required

PINK BRACELET

- *7.6m (25ft) enamelled wire in vivid pink*
- *roughly 25 faceted beads in vivid pink*
- *roughly 8 round beads in iridescent pink*
- *wire cutters*

To achieve even results, always tie the knots in the same way and adjust the loops with your fingers as you go.

> **You can personalize your designs** by choosing a coloured wire to match the beads you have at home.

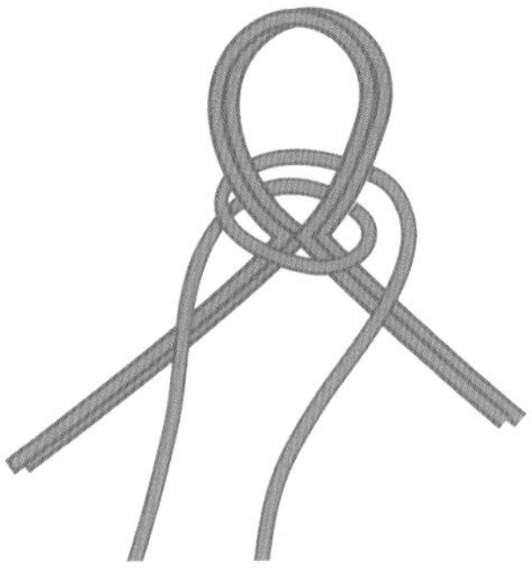

❶ To obtain the side wires, take two 3.5m ($11^1/_2$ft) lengths of pink wire and bring them together. Halve them and make a small loop at the middle point which will act as the buttonhole (ensure that the size of the loop matches the button bead). Next, take a 60cm (24in) length of pink wire and halve it, this is the base wire. At this middle point wind the wire twice around the loop to secure.

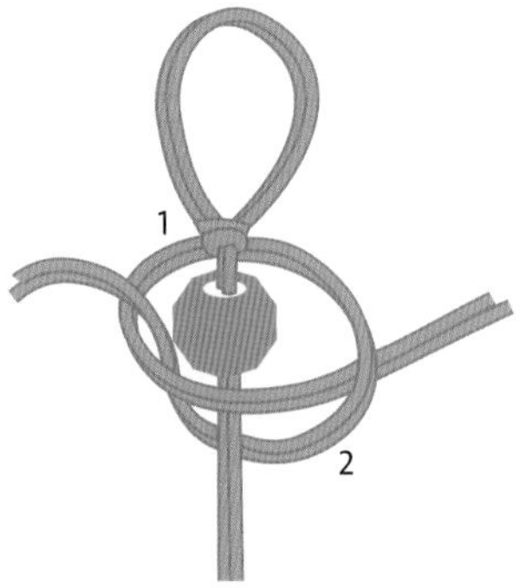
1
2

❷ Thread a pink faceted bead on to the base wires, sliding the bead as far as the button loop. Tie a knot with the side wires, taking the left wire over the front and right wire around the back, and tie them around the bead.

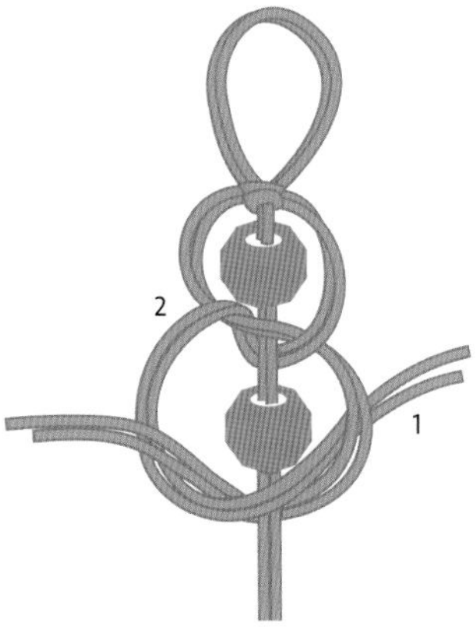
2
1

❸ Thread a second pink bead on to the wires and tie the same knot, starting this time with the right-hand wires. Repeat over roughly 18cm (7in), alternating three pink faceted beads and one round iridescent bead.

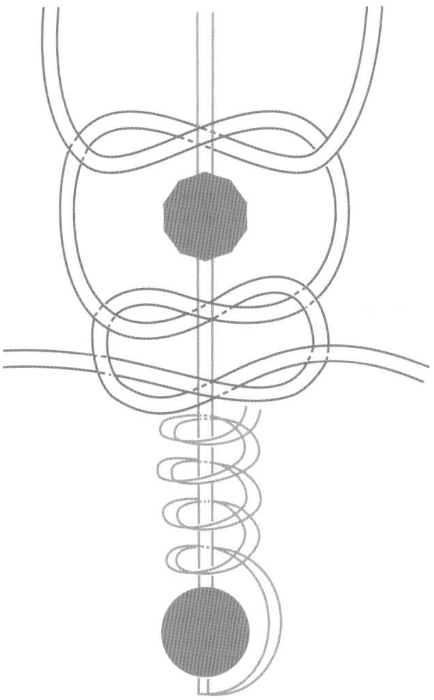

❹ To finish off, tie two knots one on top of the other but without threading on any beads, then thread on the button bead. Bend the wires back over the bead and wind them tightly four times behind the bead. Trim the excess wire using wire cutters.

Materials required

TURQUOISE RING

- *2m (6ft 7in) enamelled wire in turquoise blue*
- *roughly 20 faceted beads in turquoise blue*
- *wire cutters*

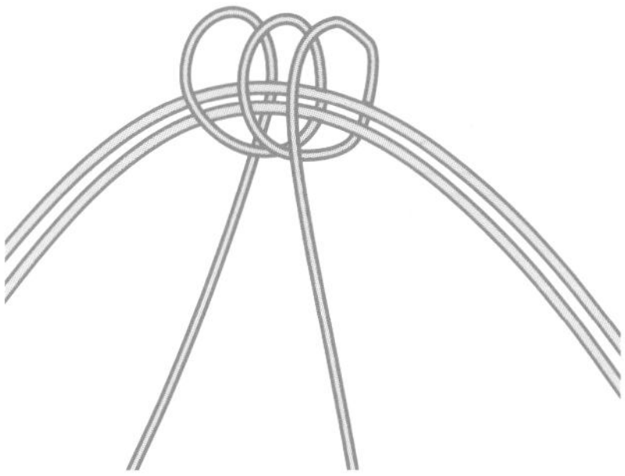

❶ To make the base wires, cut a 30cm (12in) length of turquoise enamelled wire and halve it to determine its middle point. Take the remaining wire and halve it to determine its middle point, then wind the middle point of the base wires tightly around that point three times.

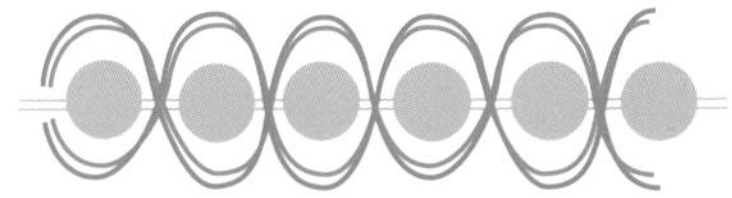

❷ Thread a blue bead on to the base wires and push it up to the join in the wires. Tie a macramé knot, then thread on another bead (see page 28, steps 2 and 3). Continue to work in this way over roughly 6cm ($2^1/_4$in).

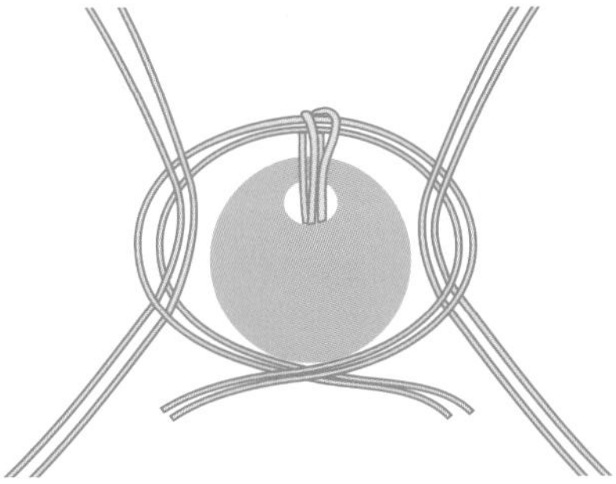

❸ To finish the ring, pass the side wires through the knot that encloses the first bead in the ring then make a knot with the base wires and the side wires. Tighten, then trim the excess wire.

Materials required

DOUBLE ORANGE BRACELET

- *15.2m (50ft) enamelled wire in orange*
- *about 60 orange faceted beads and 15 brown*
- *1 large bead in orange*
- *wire cutters*

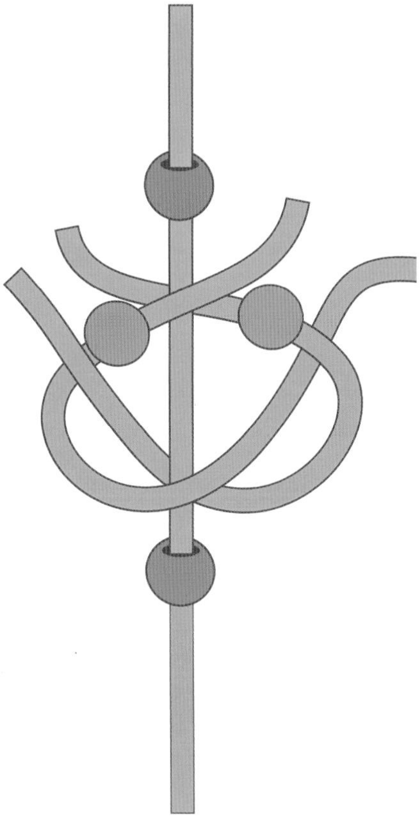

1 Cut a 1.2m (4ft) length of orange wire and halve it to make the base wires. To make the side wires, take the remainder of the wire and halve it to determine the middle point. Make and secure a button loop following the technique for Pink Bracelet (see page 28, step 1).

2 Follow the instructions for the Pink Bracelet (see page 28, steps 2 and 3), using a single brown bead on the base wire and two orange beads on the side wires. The beads are threaded on before the base wire is knotted. Alternate the beads as follows: two orange beads on the side wires; one brown bead in the centre; one loop with no beads. Continue to work in this way over roughly 38cm (15in).

3 To finish off, thread on the button bead and secure (see page 28, step 4).

Feather and Bead Designs

Materials required

PINK AND BLUE NECKLACES

- *small glass beads in blue, pink, iridescent pink, iridescent blue, pale mauve and pale pink*
- *small or large sequins in blue, purple and salmon pink*
- *faceted beads in a variety of sizes, in blue, mauve, purple, pink, pale pink, iridescent pink and clear blue and pink*
- *flat beads in blue and pink*
- *droplet and crystal beads in blue and pink*
- *bugles in blue and pink*
- *feathers in pink and midnight blue*
- *round beads in pale pink, violet, iridescent pink and iridescent blue*
- *coloured wire*
- *crimp beads*
- *flat-nosed pliers*
- *cylindrical metal necklace clasp*
- *wire cutters*

SET OF EARRINGS

- *pink feathers*
- *2 flat beads in pale pink*
- *2 large beads in iridescent pink*
- *large sequins in pink*
- *crimp beads*
- *2 earring rings and findings*
- *pink wire*
- *flat-nosed pliers*

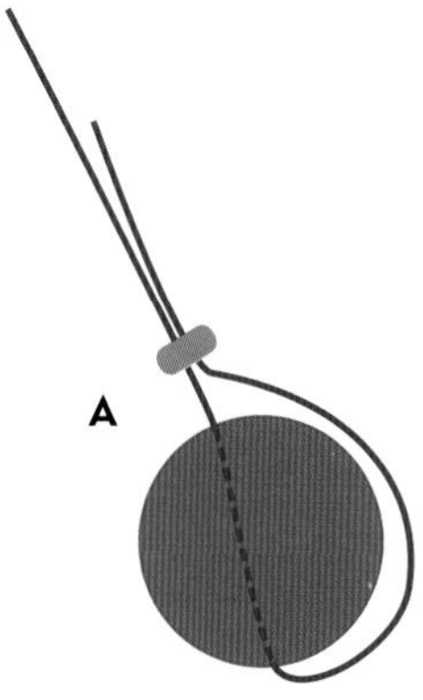
A

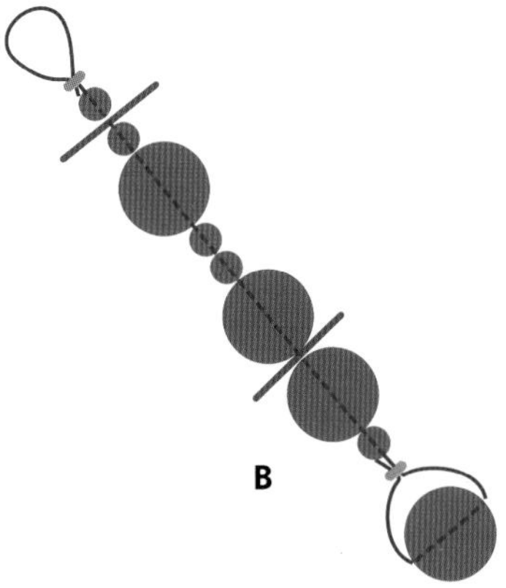
B

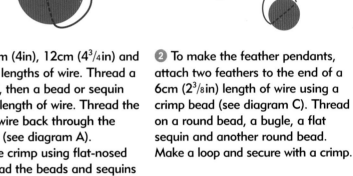

1 Cut 10cm (4in), 12cm (4¾in) and 15cm (6in) lengths of wire. Thread a crimp bead, then a bead or sequin on to each length of wire. Thread the end of the wire back through the crimp bead (see diagram A). Squeeze the crimp using flat-nosed pliers. Thread the beads and sequins on to the wire in random order, alternating colours and shapes, and finish with a crimp bead. Make a loop at the end of the pendant and thread the wire back into the crimp bead (see diagram B). Squeeze the bead and trim the excess wire. Make up 13 different pendants, aiming for an even distribution of shapes and colours.

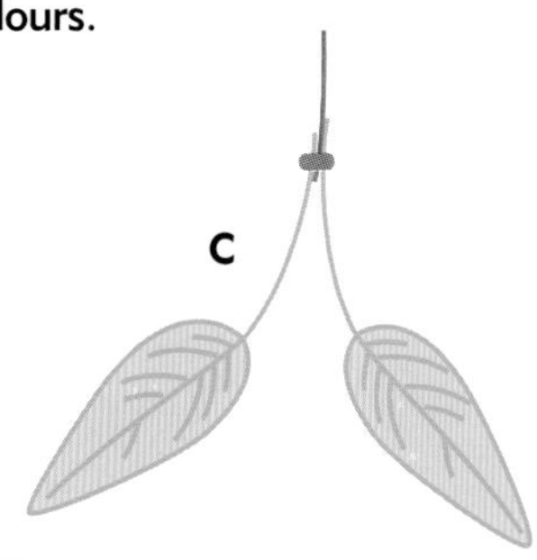
C

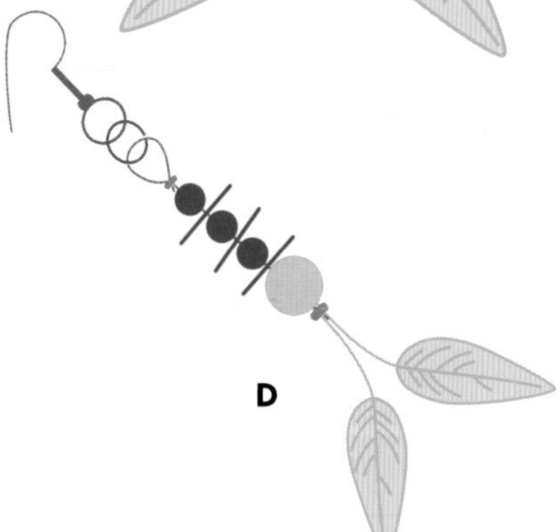
D

2 To make the feather pendants, attach two feathers to the end of a 6cm (2⅜in) length of wire using a crimp bead (see diagram C). Thread on a round bead, a bugle, a flat sequin and another round bead. Make a loop and secure with a crimp.

3 Lie the pendants out and arrange them in a finished design. Cut a 38cm (15in) length of wire. Thread the pendants on to it, starting at the centre of the necklace and threading on a bead between each one. Finish the ends of the necklace with a variety of different beads and attach the cylindrical clasp (see page 22, step 3).

4 **To make the earrings:** work in the same way as the feather pendant: attach two feathers to the end of a 6cm (2⅜in) length of wire using a crimp bead. Thread on your chosen beads. Add a crimp bead, then thread on the earring ring. Thread the wire back into the crimp bead and squeeze with the pliers to close (see diagram D). Attach the earring findings.

Rustic Clay Necklace ★★

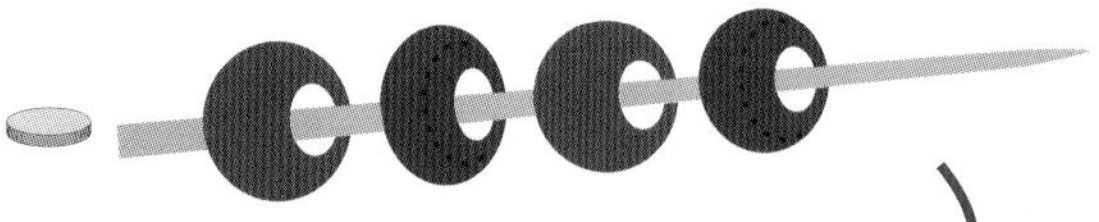

Materials required

TURQUOISE NECKLACE

- *3 lengths of leather thonging: 2 blue, 1 turquoise*
- *red air-drying clay*
- *skewers*
- *5 silver fish-shaped beads*
- *3 silver star-shaped charms*
- *20 novelty beads in turquoise*

1. Using the red air-drying clay make a selection of round beads (about the size of a hazelnut), small cylindrical beads, flat beads and small round beads so that you have 16 beads plus one extra to fasten the necklace. Wet the ends of your fingers with a little water and thread 4 or 5 beads on a skewer. Prick every other bead with another skewer to decorate. Leave to dry for a day.

2. Thread a bead into the centre of a length of leather thonging and tie a small knot on either side of it. Thread a bead on either side of the centre bead and tie two small knots. Continue to work in this way over roughly 21cm ($8\frac{1}{4}$in), varying the shape and colour of bead. Repeat on the remaining lengths of leather thonging.

Thin leather thonging is quite fragile, so take care not to pull too hard on the thread when knotting.

> **To make a green necklace,** use three lengths of green leather thonging (one pale green and two dark green), some green air-drying clay, six large decorated silver beads, nine silver charms, fourteen mother-of-pearl beads (flowers and leaves) and seven small pierced white shells.
>
> **To make an orange necklace,** use three lengths of leather thonging (orange, pink and red), some red and yellow air-drying clay and 100 small wooden beads in yellow, red, orange and pink.

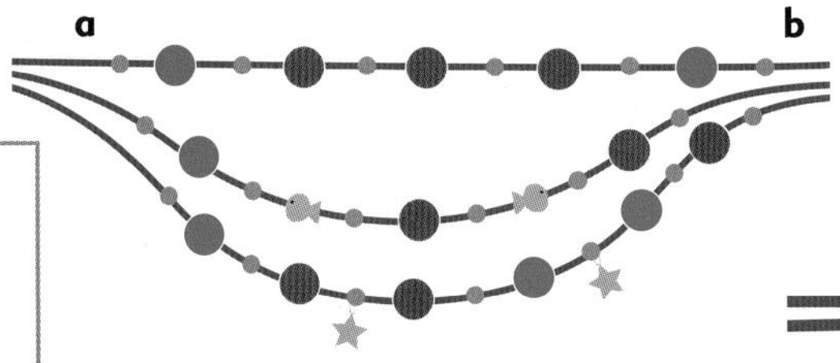
a
b

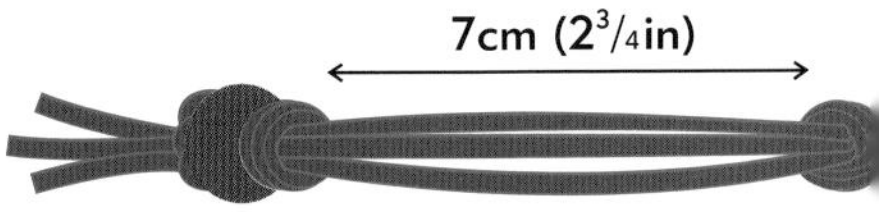
7cm (2³/4in)

3. Lay the three lengths of leather thonging together as shown above. Knot them together 1cm ($\frac{3}{8}$in) from the last knot on the top row (see point a and b above).

4. Tie the thonging in another knot 7cm ($2\frac{3}{4}$in) from knot 'a'. Thread on a large bead and secure with another knot. Cut the thonging 3mm ($\frac{1}{8}$in) beyond this knot. At the other end make a loop the size of the large bead with one of the lengths of thonging 7cm ($2\frac{3}{4}$in) from knot 'b'. Using one of the other lengths, secure the loop with a series of blanket stitch type knots.

Disc and Flower Droplets ★★

Materials required

DISC NECKLACE

- *card*
- *pair of compasses*
- *thick plastic sheeting in purple, blue and green*
- *scissors*
- *hole punch*
- *nylon thread*
- *crimp beads*
- *flat-nosed pliers*
- *1 silver cylindrical necklace clasp*

❶ Take a piece of card and draw out three discs 2cm (¾in), 2.5cm (1in) and 3cm (1¼in) in diameter. Cut five small discs, 7 medium discs and 8 large discs from each of the coloured sheets of plastic. Pierce a small hole 3mm (⅛in) from the edge of each disc using the hole punch.

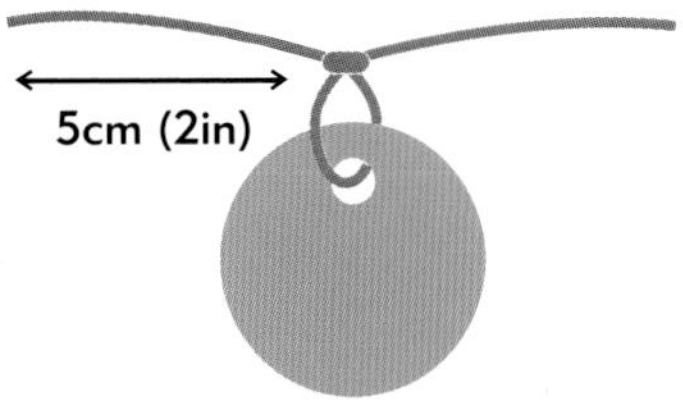
5cm (2in)

❷ Cut three 65cm (25½in) lengths of nylon. Thread on a crimp bead and a disc 5cm (2in) from the end of each length of thread. Thread the nylon back through the crimp bead to form a small loop, then squeeze the crimp.
Continue to work in this way, leaving 1–2cm (⅜–¾in) between discs and varying their sizes and colours as you go. Stop 5cm (2in) from the end of the thread.

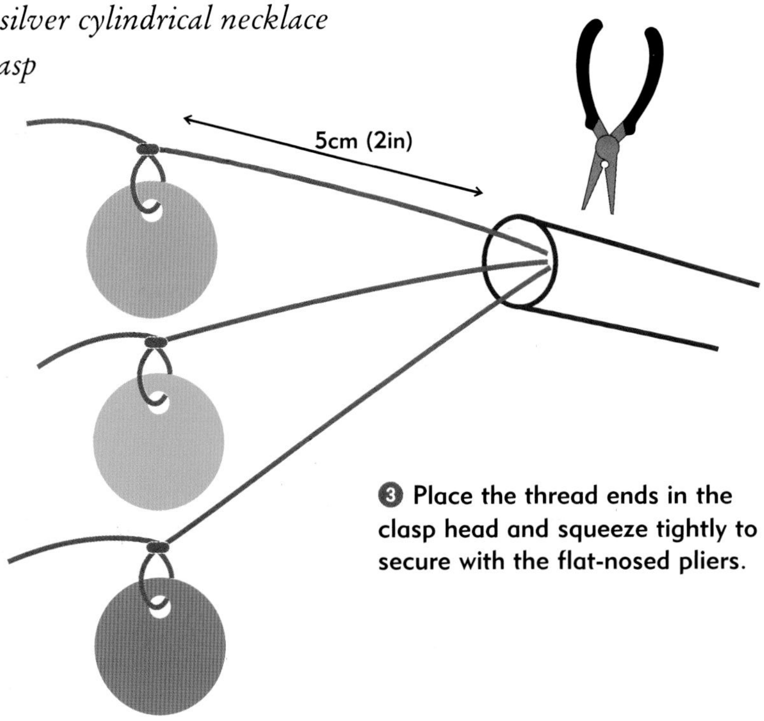
5cm (2in)

❸ Place the thread ends in the clasp head and squeeze tightly to secure with the flat-nosed pliers.

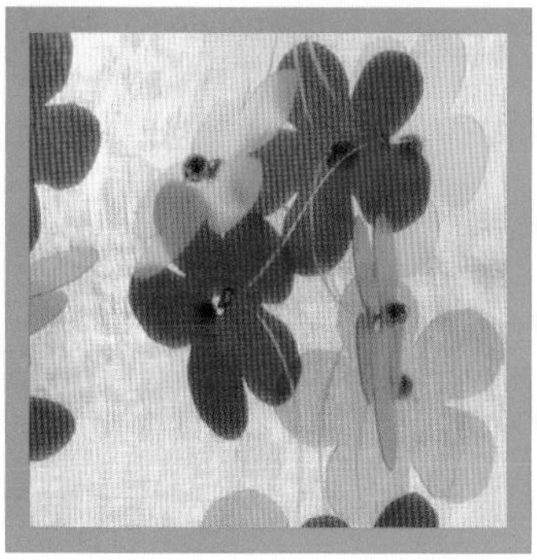

B

Materials required

FLOWER NECKLACE

- *tracing paper*
- *card*
- *thick plastic sheeting in red, yellow and orange*
- *pointed scissors*
- *hole punch*
- *nylon thread*
- *crimp beads*
- *round beads in silver*
- *flat-nosed pliers*
- *1 silver cylindrical necklace clasp*

1 Trace over flower A below, transfer to card and use as a template. Cut out 18 red, 18 yellow and 18 orange flowers from the plastic sheeting. Make a hole in the centre of each flower with the hole punch.

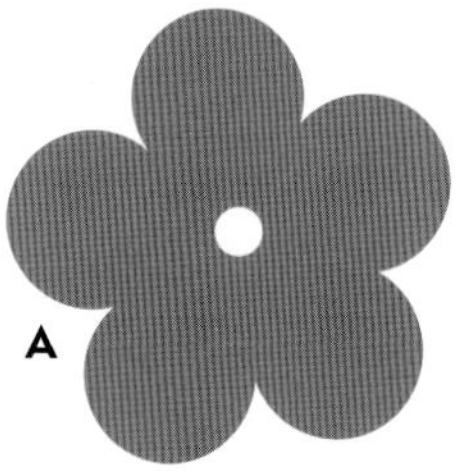
A

2 Cut three 65cm (25½in) lengths of nylon. Thread on a crimp bead, a flower and a silver bead 5cm (2in) from the end of each length of thread. Pass the thread back into the flower, then into the crimp (see diagram B). Squeeze the crimp bead using the flat-nosed pliers. Continue to work in this way, leaving 1–2cm (⅜–¾in) between flowers and alternating the colours as you go. Stop 5cm (2in) from the ends of the thread.

3 Place the thread ends in the clasp heads and squeeze tightly with flat-nosed pliers to secure.

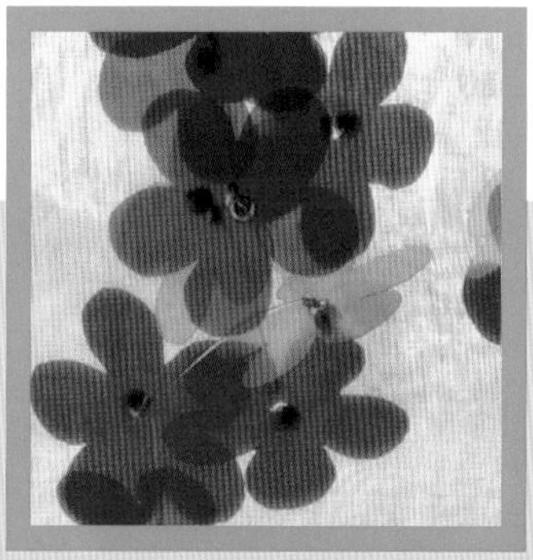

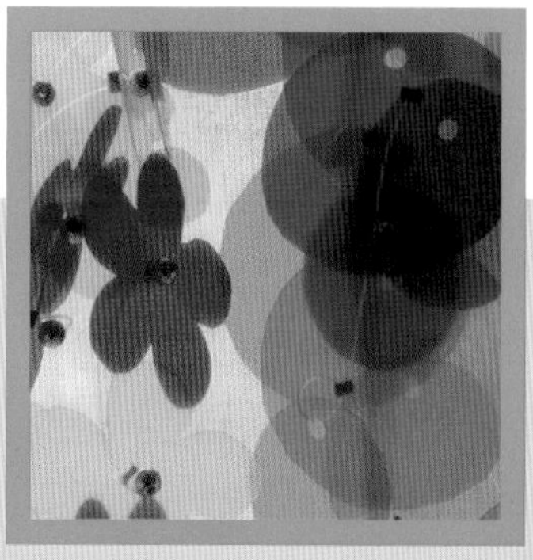

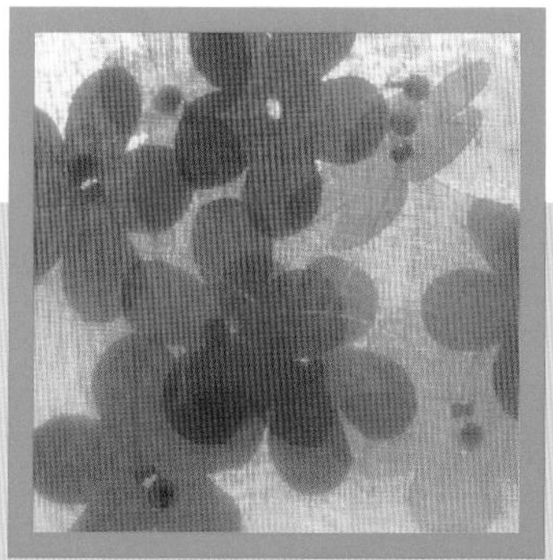

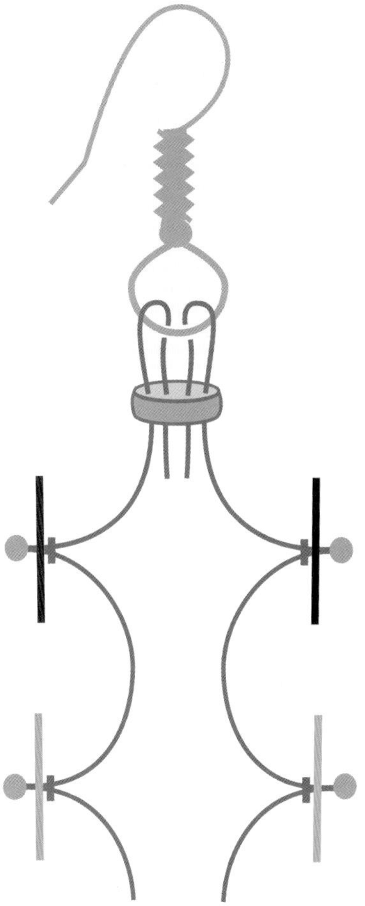

Materials required

FLOWER EARRINGS

- *thick plastic sheeting in purple, orange and red*
- *scissors*
- *hole punch*
- *nylon thread*
- *crimp beads*
- *round beads in silver*
- *flat-nosed pliers*
- *earring findings*

1 Use the flower template (see page 38, diagram A) and cut out 6 purple flowers, 7 orange and 7 red flowers from the plastic sheeting. Make a hole in the centre of each flower with the hole punch.

2 Cut four 15cm (6in) lengths of nylon and use two threads to make up each earring. Decorate each thread using the same technique as for the Flower Necklace (see page 38, step 2). Vary the colours of the flowers on each thread.

3 **To attach the earring finding:** take the ends of two of the decorated threads. Thread a crimp bead on to the two threads, pass the ends into the loop of the earring finding and thread them back into the crimp bead. Squeeze tight with flat-nosed pliers. Trim the excess thread at both ends.

Fringed Necklace ★★

Materials required

GREEN NECKLACE

- *bugles in bright green*
- *40cm (16in) length of 1cm (3/8in) wide velvet ribbon in matching green*
- *green thread*
- *a fine needle*
- *small glass beads in pale, opaque and clear green*
- *small glass beads in dark orange or brown*
- *faceted beads in pale green*
- *round beads in polished glass and matt green*
- *sequins in green and brown*
- *2 flat ends in gold*
- *2 gold rings*
- *1 gold clasp*
- *flat-nosed pliers*

To make a hairclip, take an 8cm ($3^1/_8$in) hairclip mount and a piece of maroon felt 8 x 1.5cm ($3^1/_8$ x $^5/_8$in). Sew the bugles on to the lower edge of the piece of felt. Make up the fringes so that they come out from every bugle rather than every other bugle, and sew on three rows of small glass beads above the bugles. Stick to the mount with strong glue.

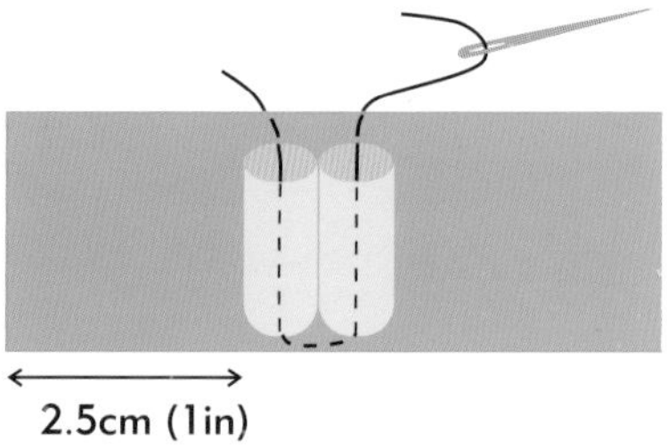
2.5cm (1in)

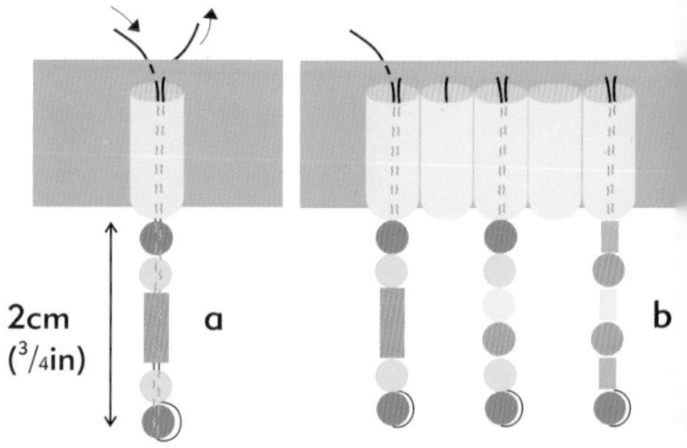
2cm
($^3/_4$in)
a
b

1 Start working 2.5cm (1in) from the end of the ribbon. Using the green thread and needle, sew the bugles on side by side along the lower edge of the ribbon over 35cm ($13^3/_4$in), following the diagram above. Finish with a stitch on the wrong side of the ribbon.

2 To make the fringes, tie a knot in the end of the thread, bring the needle through from the wrong side of the ribbon and take through the first bugle. Thread on roughly 2cm ($^3/_4$in) of beads, varying the shapes and colours used. Go back over the final bead and back through the other beads, then into the bugle. Take the needle back through to the reverse of the ribbon and back out at the next but one bugle. Repeat this process on every other bugle.

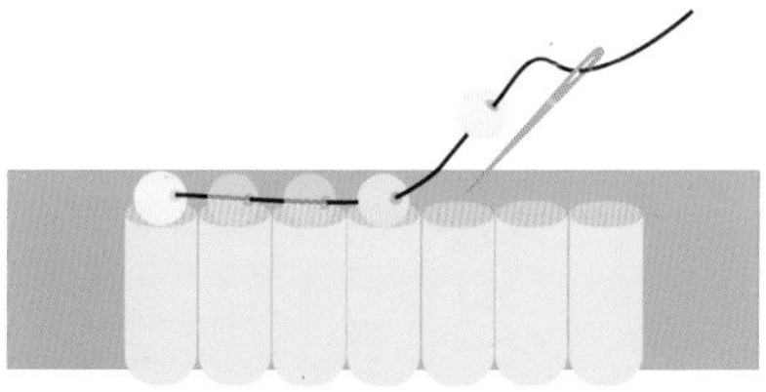

3 Sew a row of small glass beads along the upper edge of the ribbon above the bugles, using opaque and clear beads.

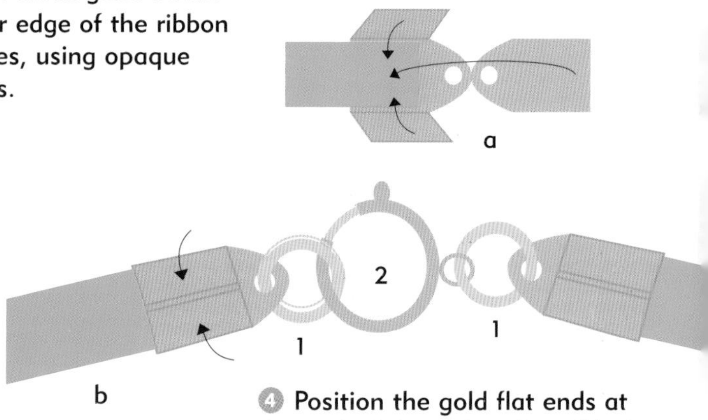
a
2
1
1
b

4 Position the gold flat ends at the end of the ribbon 2cm ($^3/_4$in) from the last bead, then assemble the rings and clasp, following the diagrams above as a guide.

Tubular Jewellery ★★

Materials required

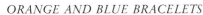

ORANGE AND BLUE BRACELETS

- *plastic tubing in fuchsia, pink, orange and yellow, or pink, purple, pale green and sky-blue*
- *elasticated nylon thread*
- *a fine needle*
- *needle-threader*

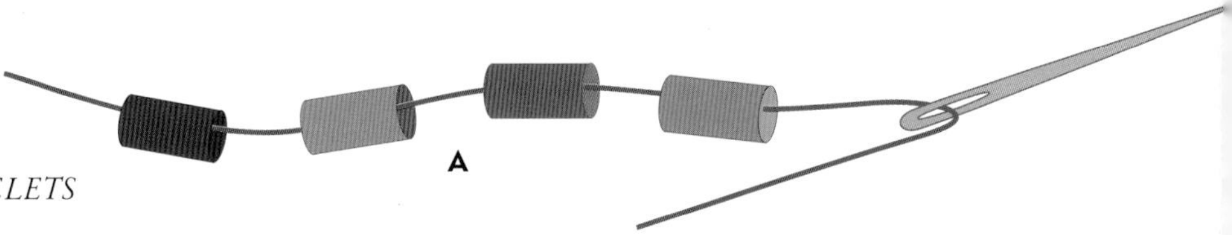

A

1. Cut the plastic tubing into 1.5cm (5/8in) pieces. Cut a 1.5m (4ft 11in) length of elasticated nylon thread and thread it through the eye of the needle using the needle-threader.

2. Thread the pieces of plastic tubing on to the nylon thread, varying the colours as you go (see diagram A). Leave 1–2cm (3/8–3/4in) thread at both ends to fasten the bracelet.

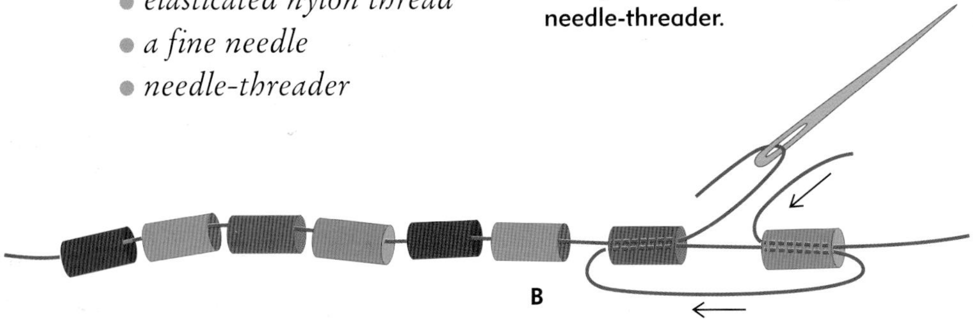

B

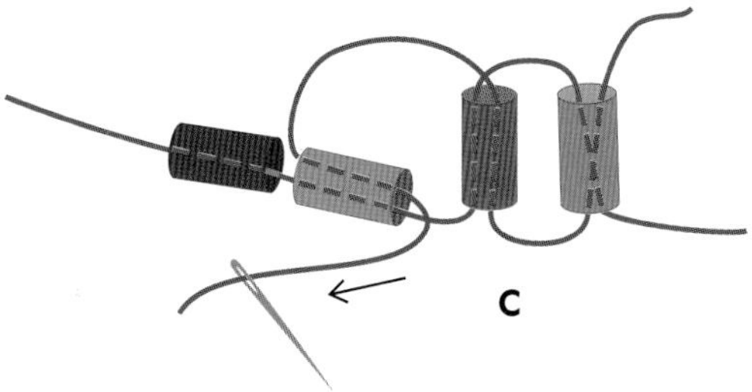

C

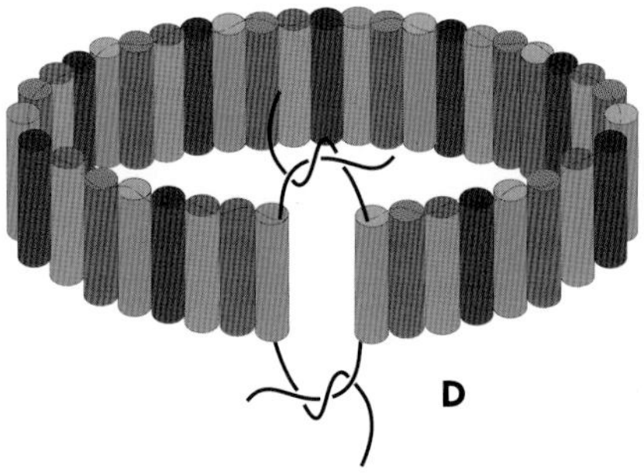

D

Ensure that you do not pull too hard on the thread: the plastic tubing pieces should sit comfortably side by side without overlapping.

Use the same technique to make an original bracelet by alternating between plastic tubing and small glass beads.

3. Cut a 2m (6ft 7in) length of elasticated nylon thread, and thread it through the needle. Thread it through the first piece of plastic tubing left to right, then into the next piece of tubing right to left and pull the tubing upright. Repeat this process until you reach the end (see diagrams B and C).

4. Bring the two ends of the bracelet together and tie a tight double knot. Trim the excess thread.

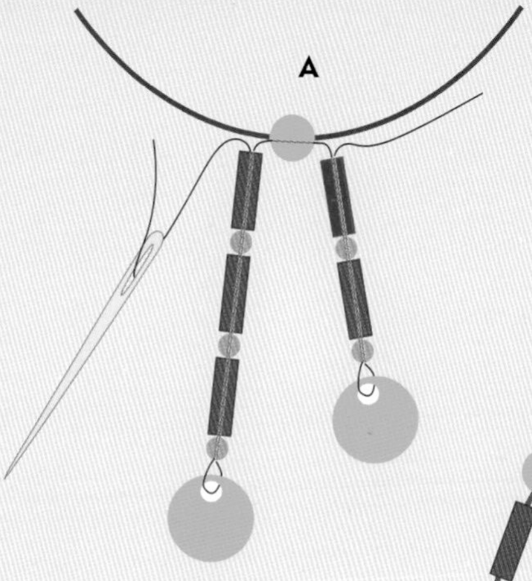
A

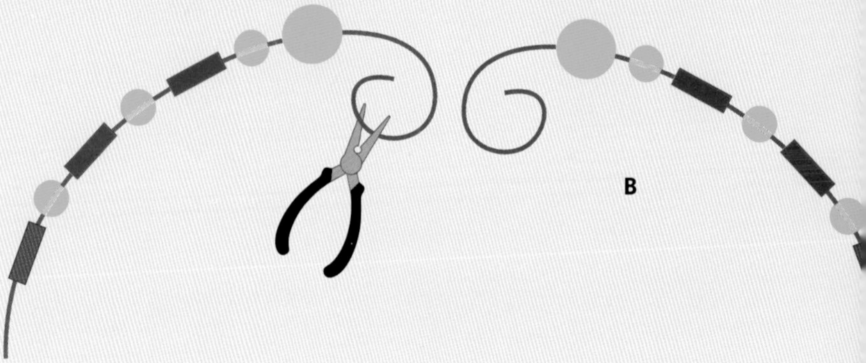
B

Materials required

SPRUNG WIRE NECKLACE

- *1 metal sprung necklace wire*
- *plastic tubing in pale pink, deep pink and mauve*
- *pink thread*
- *a fine needle*
- *small clear glass beads in pink*
- *sequins with side holes in pink and purple*
- *2 large pink beads*
- *round-nosed pliers*

To create a sprung wire bracelet, use small glass beads in turquoise, plastic tubing in mauve, purple and turquoise, and sequins with side holes in purple and pink. Thread the beads on, alternating them every so often with sequins. Fasten the bracelet by making a loop in the wire.

1. Cut the plastic tubing into roughly 120 x 1cm (3/8in) lengths. Using the pink thread and a needle, knot the thread around the middle point of the necklace wire. Thread on tubing and beads and finish with a sequin. Take the needle back through the beads (see diagram A). Thread a bead on to the sprung wire, take the needle and thread through the bead and make the next pendant. Repeat this pattern over 5cm (2in) on either side of the middle point.

2. On each side of the pendants, thread on alternately plastic tubing and beads. Stop 2cm (3/4in) from each end of the necklace wire.

3. Thread a large bead on to each end, then, using your round-nosed pliers, make a loop to fasten the necklace (see diagram B).

Cut 19 pieces of plastic tubing 2cm (3/4in) in length and thread them on to a 1m (39in) length of elasticated nylon thread, alternating each one with 10 small glass beads (see diagram above). Take a second length of elasticated nylon thread back through the tubing and beads to make them stand up (see page 42, step 3). Glue to the hairclip mount.

Materials required

HAIRCLIP

- *8cm (3 1/8in) hairclip mount*
- *plastic tubing in pale pink and deep pink*
- *elasticated nylon thread*
- *small glass beads in mauve and pink*
- *jewellery glue*

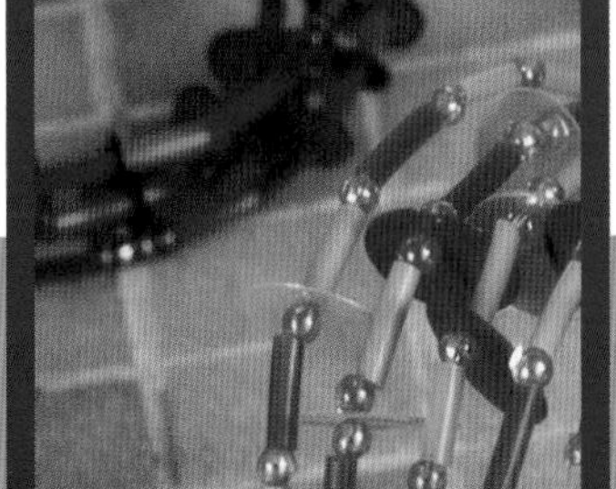

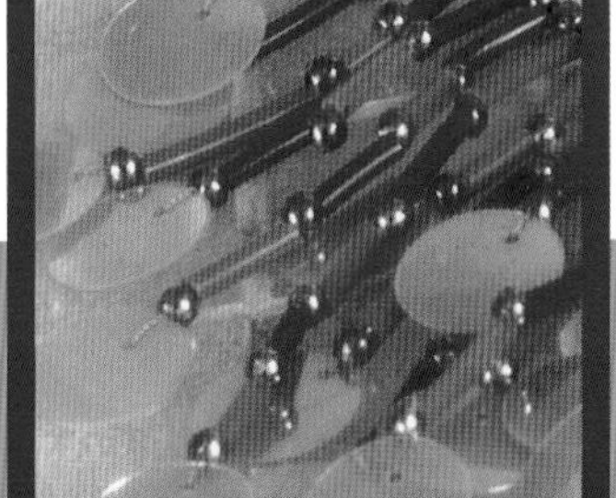

Elastic Bead Bands ★★★

Materials required

BRACELET

- *30–40 metal eye pins*
- *30 fairly large beads*
- *2–3 types of small glass bead (round/long)*
- *round-nosed pliers*
- *a needle*
- *1m (39in) elasticated thread*

Your rings should be tightly closed so as to prevent the elastic from falling out.

To work out the bead design try the combination out on at least six eye pins, then place side by side to view.

1 Decide on the bead design for the pins, then make up roughly 33 eye pins (for an 18cm ($7^1/_8$in) bracelet), by threading 2cm ($^3/_4$in) of beads on to each eye pin.

2 Cut each pin approximately 8mm ($^5/_{16}$in) from the beads and make a loop using the pliers to form a tight ring. Tighten the existing ring, too.

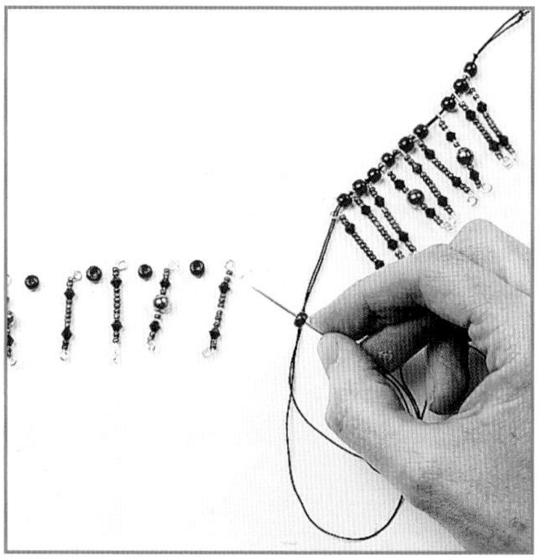

3 Thread roughly 50cm (20in) elasticated thread on to a needle, halve it and tie a knot in the end. Thread on a large bead, then an eye pin, a bead, then an eye pin. Repeat until all the eye pins are used. Repeat this process at the other end of the eye pins.

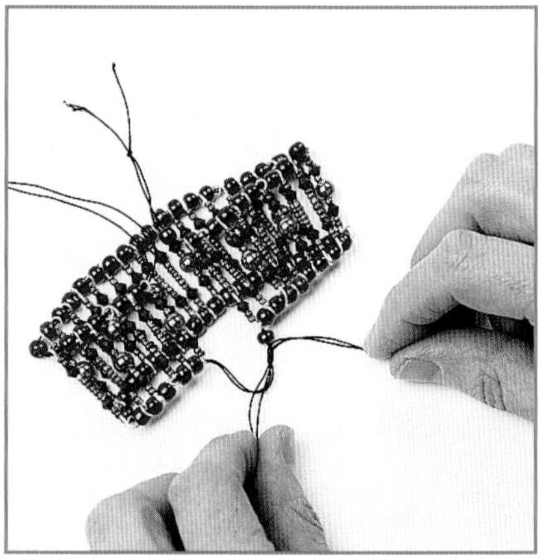

4 Bring the two ends of the bracelet together and tie two tight knots one on top of the other at top and bottom.

Woven Ribbon Jewellery ★★

Materials required

PINK BRACELET

- *1.5m (4ft 11in) length of 0.3mm ($^{1}/_{64}$in) diameter thin wire*
- *small faceted beads in purple*
- *medium faceted beads in vivid pink and mauve*
- *40cm (16in) length of 2cm ($^{3}/_{4}$in) wide sheer ribbon in deep pink*

MAUVE NECKLACE

- *1.8m (5ft 11in) of 0.3mm ($^{1}/_{64}$in) diameter thin wire*
- *small faceted beads in purple*
- *small glass beads in sky-blue*
- *90cm (35$^{1}/_{2}$in) length of 7mm ($^{1}/_{4}$in) wide sheer ribbon in mauve*

Before starting work on this project, check how wide the holes in your beads are: they should be able to contain two lengths of wire.

Colour-coordinate your jewellery by simply weaving a different coloured ribbon through the bead design.

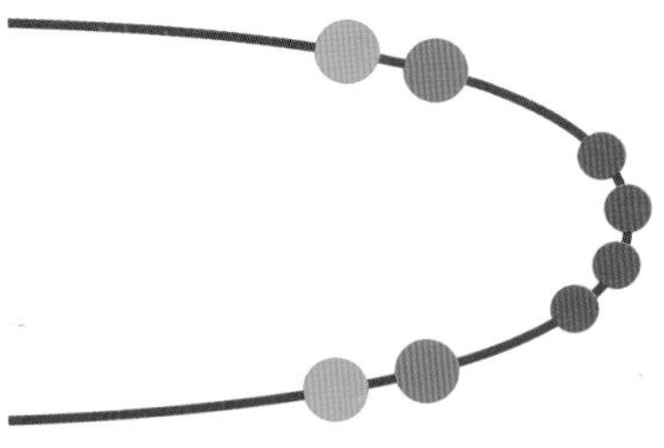

To make the bracelet

1. Thread four purple beads into the centre of the wire, then thread one mauve bead and one pink bead on each end of the wire.

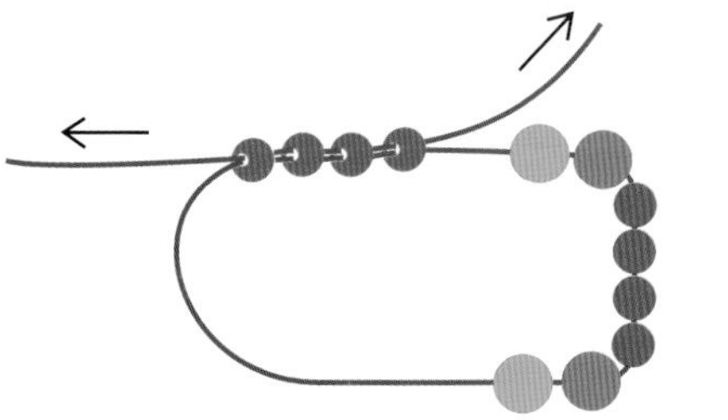

2. Now thread on four purple beads and thread the other end of the wire through these four beads in the opposite direction to the first wire. Pull on the two wires to make the row stand up vertically. Thread on two more mauve and pink beads.

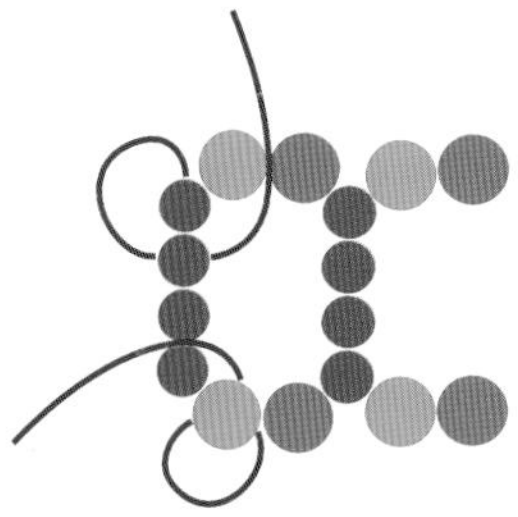

3. Repeat this process roughly 18 times, depending on the size of your wrist. Finish off by winding the wire tightly around the last vertical row three times.

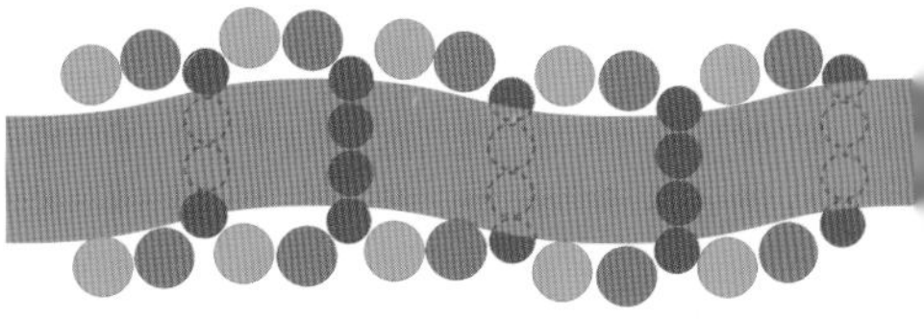

4. Weave the ribbon through the 'mesh' of the bracelet, taking it over and then under each vertical row. Leave roughly 12cm (4$^{3}/_{4}$in) excess on each side to fasten.

To make the mauve necklace

Make the mauve necklace using the same technique as the bracelet above. The vertical rows are made up of a faceted bead set between two small glass beads, and the horizontal rows are made up of two faceted beads separated by one small glass bead.
Work in the same way as for the bracelet, repeating step 2 around 36 times, depending on your neck measurement.

African-Style Pendants ★★★

Materials required

PENDANT

- *2 x 7.5cm (3in) lengths of 8mm ($^{5}/_{16}$in) diameter thick wire*
- *1.6m (5ft 3in) thin wire*
- *small glass beads in mauve, pink and iridescent pink*
- *41cm (16in) silver wire*
- *1 cylindrical necklace clasp in silver*
- *flat-nosed pliers*
- *round-nosed pliers*

For a rounded finish, take care not to pull too hard on the wire when threading the beads around the cross.

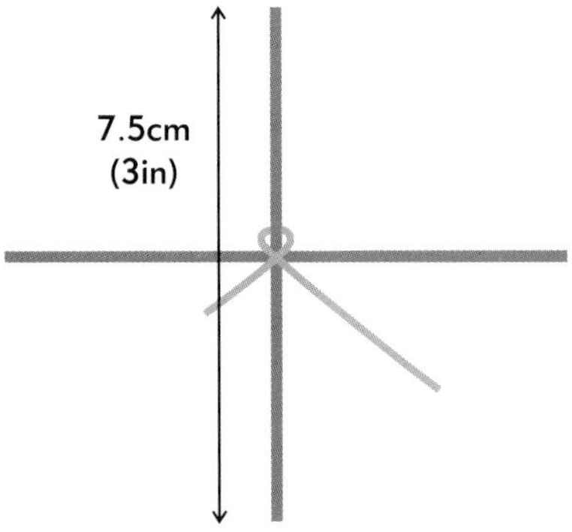
7.5cm
(3in)

1 To make a 7cm ($2^{3}/_{4}$in) disc make a cross with the two lengths of thick wire and secure by winding the end of the thin wire around them at their centre.

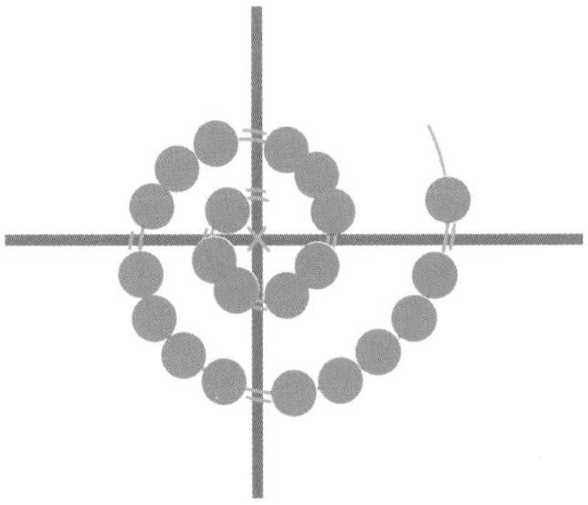

2 Thread two mauve beads on to the thin wire and wind the wire once around one arm of the cross. Thread on two more mauve beads and wind the wire around the second arm and so on until you complete the fourth arm. Wind four more rows of mauve beads, increasing the number of beads by one each time you go around the cross. Then wind on three circles of pink beads and five circles of iridescent pink beads.

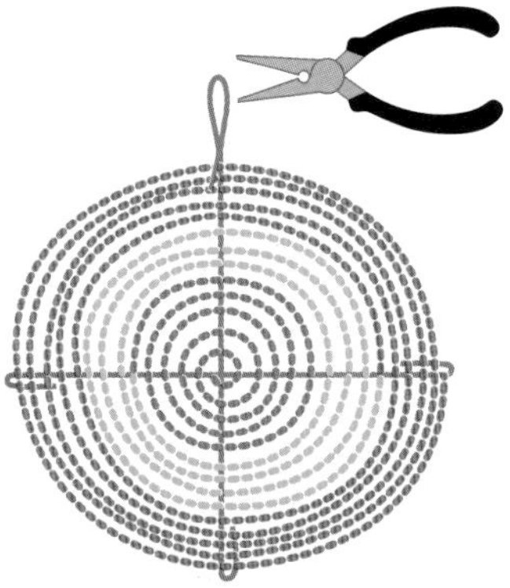

3 To finish off, wind the thin wire several times around one of the arms of the cross and trim the excess. Bend and flatten down the ends of three arms of the cross towards the back of the disc using the flat-nosed pliers. To make the necklace attachment, make a small, very narrow loop (smaller than the diameter of a bead) with the last of the arms using the round-nosed pliers.

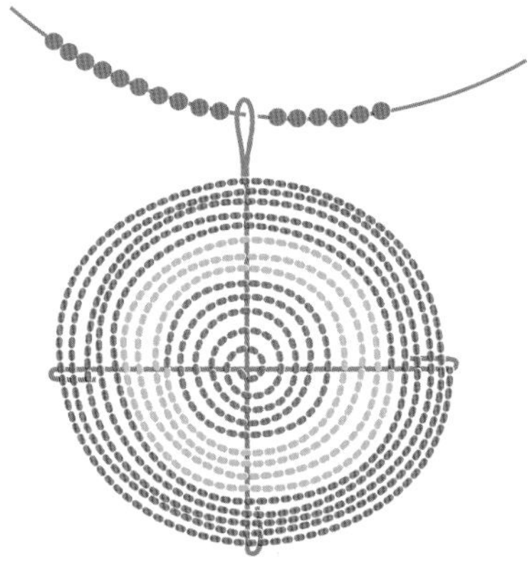

4 To assemble the necklace, thread the pendant on to the centre of the silver wire, then thread mauve beads either side of it. Secure the ends of the silver wire in the clasps and squeeze tight with flat-nosed pliers.

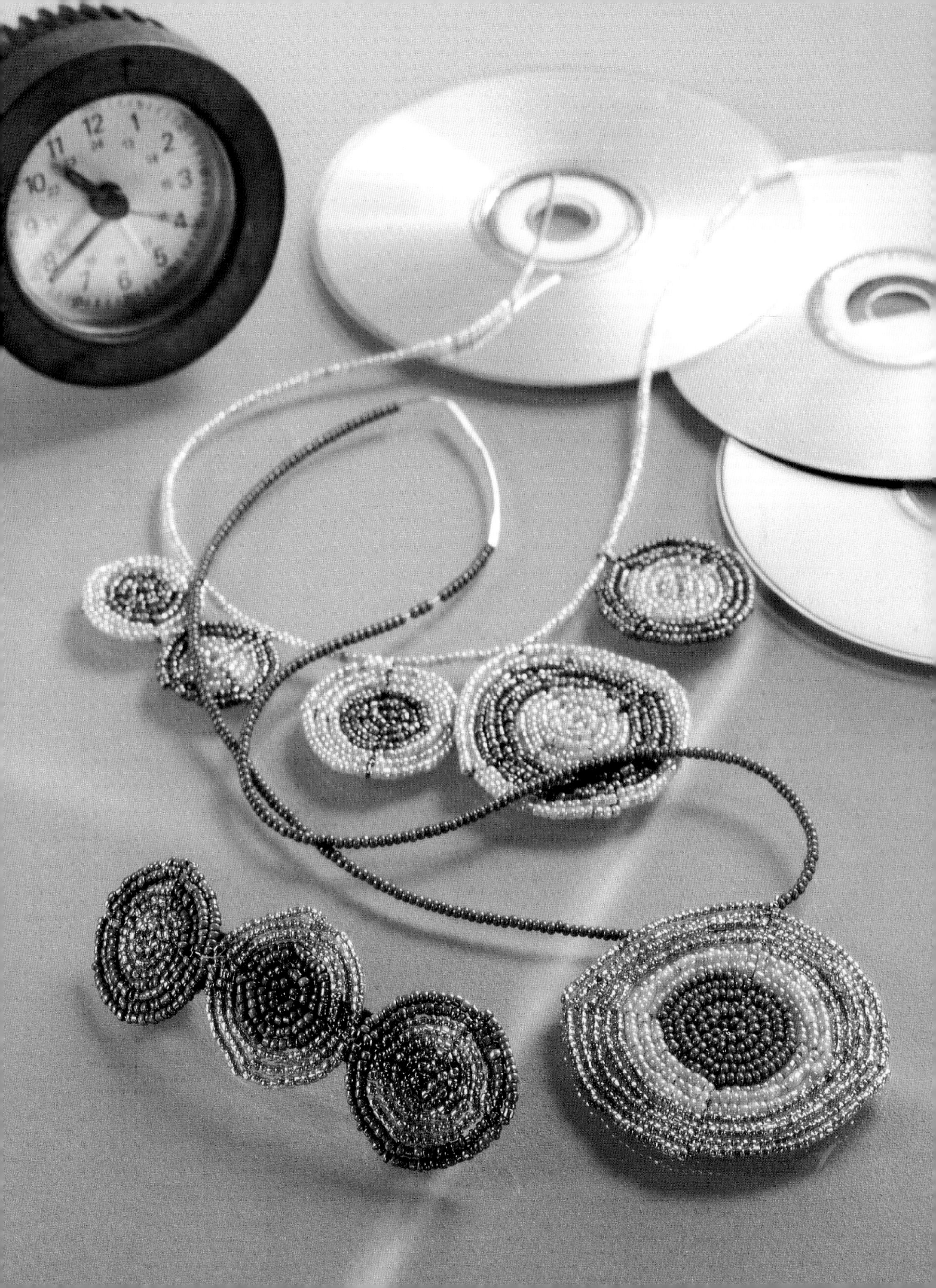

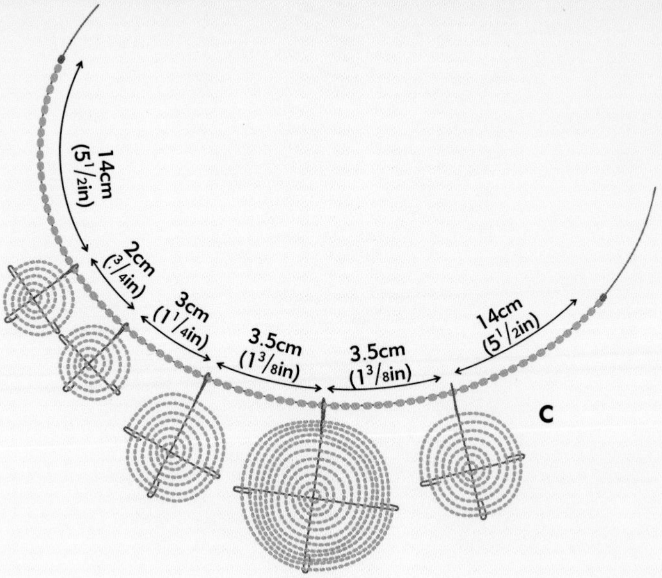
14cm (5 1/2in)
2cm (3/4in)
3cm (1 1/4in)
3.5cm (1 3/8in)
3.5cm (1 3/8in)
14cm (5 1/2in)
C

Materials required

PENDANT NECKLACE

- *small glass beads in blue and green*
- *thick wire, 0.8mm (1/32in) in diameter*
- *thin wire*
- *flat-nosed pliers*
- *round-nosed pliers*
- *silver wire*
- *1 cylindrical necklace clasp in silver*

Follow the instructions for the Pendant (see page 50) to make up the discs for this necklace.

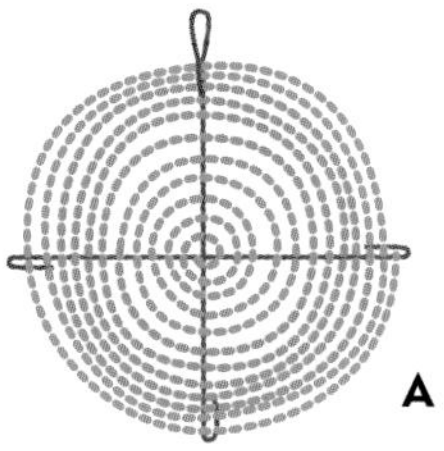
A

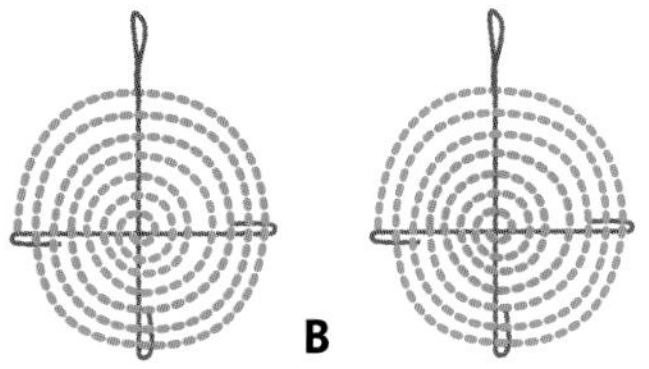
B

1 To make the large 5cm (2in) disc, make a cross out of two 7cm (2 3/4in) lengths of thick wire. Use 1m (39in) of thin wire to secure. Make five circles of blue beads, four circles of green beads and another two circles of blue beads.

2 For two 3.5cm (1 3/8in) discs make crosses out of two 4cm (1 5/8in) lengths of thick wire. Use 60cm (24in) of thin wire to secure. Make up four circles of green beads and three circles of blue beads. Thread the beads on with the colours the other way around to make the second disc.

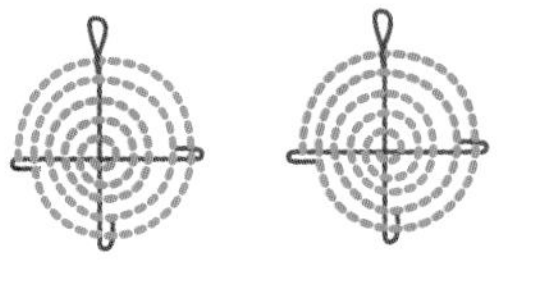

3 To make up two 2.5cm (1in) discs, make the crosses out of two 3cm (1 1/4in) lengths of thick wire. Use 50cm (20in) of thin wire to secure. Make up three circles of green beads and two circles of blue beads for the first disc, and thread the colours on in reverse order to make up the second disc.

4 Cut a 41cm (16in) length of silver wire. Thread the necklace in the following order: 14cm (5 1/2in) blue beads, one of the medium-sized discs, 3.5cm (1 3/8in) beads, the largest disc, 3.5cm (1 3/8in) beads, the second medium-sized disc, 3cm (1 1/4in) beads, one of the small discs, 2cm (3/4in) beads, the second small disc and finish off with 14cm (5 1/2in) blue beads.
The discs should not overlap (see diagram C). Secure the ends of the silver wire in the clasps and squeeze tight with the flat-nosed pliers.

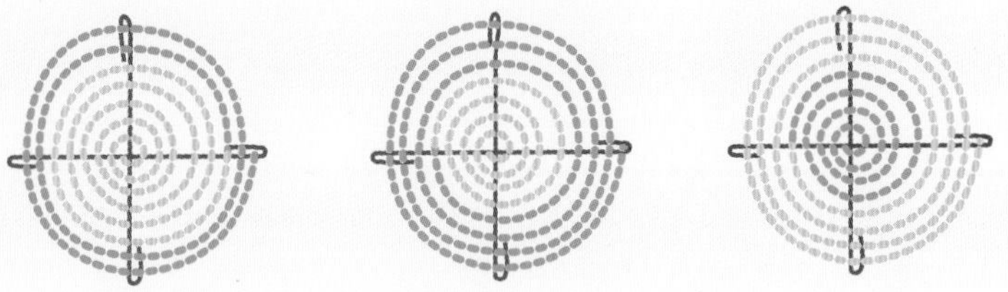

Follow the instructions for the Pendant (see page 50) to make up the discs.

1 Make up three 3.5cm (1 3/8in) pendants (see page 52, step 2). Decorate the first disc with five circles of iridescent pink beads and two circles of green beads. Decorate the second with four circles of green beads and three circles of iridescent pink beads, and the third with three circles of iridescent pink beads and four circles of green beads.

2 Glue the three discs on to the felt with strong glue, then stick the felt on to the hairclip mount.

Materials required

HAIRCLIP

- *small glass beads in iridescent pink and green*
- *thick wire, 0.8mm (1/32in) in diameter*
- *thin wire*
- *flat-nosed pliers*
- *round-nosed pliers*
- *8cm (3 1/8in) hairclip mount*
- *8 x 1.5cm (3 1/8 x 5/8in) piece of felt*
- *strong metal glue*

Ethnic Wraps ★

Materials required

NECKLACE AND MATCHING BRACELET

- *small glass beads in matt black and white*
- *black thread*
- *a fine needle*
- *3 x 47cm (18½in) lengths rubber tubing, 6mm (¼in) in diameter, for the necklace*
- *23cm (9in) length rubber tubing, 1cm (⅜in) in diameter, for the bracelet*
- *2 silver eye pins*
- *2 silver end caps*
- *2 silver rings*
- *silver clasp*
- *strong, fast-acting glue*
- *round- and flat-nosed pliers*

Design ideas: first experiment to see how many beads are needed to make a circle around the tubing: roughly 20 for the necklace and 15 for the bracelet. Try these ideas:

- 8 circles of white beads and 8 circles of black beads
- 16 circles of black beads and 1 circle of white beads
- 2 circles of white beads and 2 circles of black beads

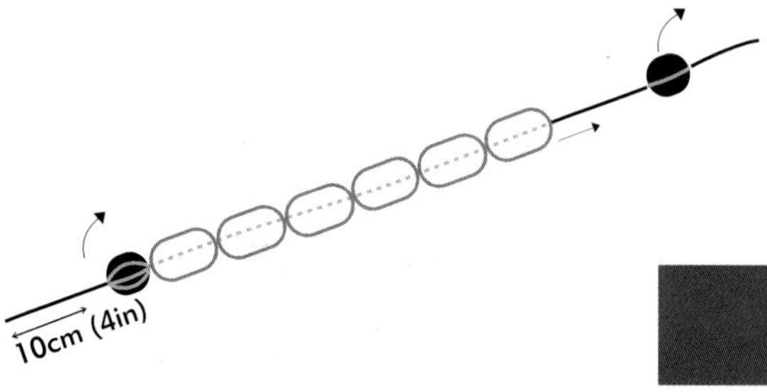
10cm (4in)

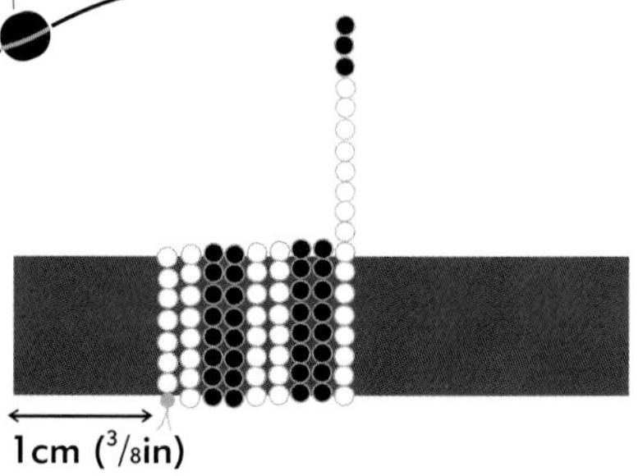
1cm (⅜in)

To make the necklace

❶ Thread the needle with 1.5m (4ft 11in) of black thread. Thread on one black bead to 10cm (4in) from the end of the thread. Secure the bead by running the thread over and through it three times. Thread on the black and white beads (see design box, below left). Stop 20cm (8in) from the end of the thread. Take the thread over and back through the last bead, without pulling too tightly – you may have to move it later.

❷ Apply a small amount of glue 1cm (⅜in) from the end of a necklace tube; glue the first few beads down, then continue to wind the beads around the tube. The beads will tighten as you wind; so in order not to break the thread, and to keep everything supple, allow some slack every so often by sliding the last bead along the black thread. Finish off 1cm (⅜in) from the end of the tube. Decorate the two other tubes in this way, varying the designs if desired.

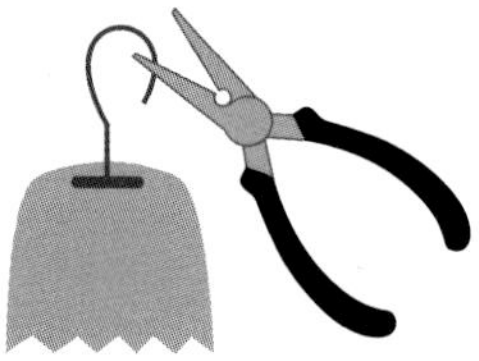

❸ To assemble the clasp, thread an eye pin through each end cap from the inside, trim the end to 1.5cm (⅝in), and make a ring using the round-nosed pliers. Thread the three tube ends into an end cap. Secure the tubing with glue and leave to dry for at least 10 minutes. Wrap the three necklaces around each other and secure the other ends in the remaining end cap. Attach the silver rings to the eye pins with flat-nosed pliers and the clasp to one of the rings.

To make the bracelet

Cut the ends of the bracelet tubing on the diagonal and glue them together. Leave to dry. Decorate the bracelet, following the same instructions as for the necklace.

Handmade Paper Beads ★

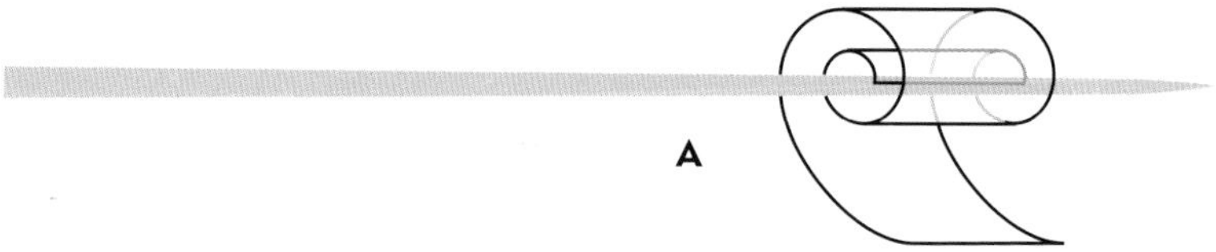

A

Materials required

BRACELET AND NECKLACE

- *wallpaper adhesive*
- *newspaper*
- *tissue paper in fuchsia, orange and plum*
- *small wooden skewers*
- *vaseline*
- *acrylic paint in gold and white*
- *medium and fine paintbrushes*
- *elasticated thread in gold, 60cm (24in) for a bracelet, 120cm (4ft) for a necklace*

1 Prepare a small amount of wallpaper adhesive following the manufacturer's instructions. Following the grain of the paper, tear off roughly 1 x 15cm ($^3/_8$ x 6in) strips of newspaper and tissue paper.

2 Coat two skewers with a thin layer of vaseline. Coat a strip of newspaper with a little wallpaper adhesive and wind it around the skewer. Add more until it is the thickness of a bead. Mould the bead as you work to form a smooth and even shape. Remove the skewer and thread the bead on to another greased skewer to dry. To make a bracelet, make 11 large beads (the size of small cherries) and 2 small beads. For the necklace, make 22 large beads and 2 small beads.

To make your beads more hard-wearing, coat them with a spray varnish.

The grain of the paper depends on how it was manufactured. Tearing the paper along the grain will give you even strips. Try it out for yourself – you will soon see which is the right way to tear.

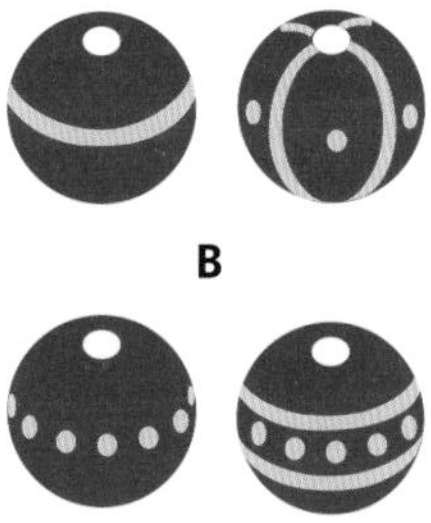

B

3 Paint the beads with a thin layer of white paint. When dry, cover them with one or two layers of tissue paper coated in glue. Smooth them over carefully and leave to dry on the skewer. Paint delicate patterns on the beads with gold acrylic.

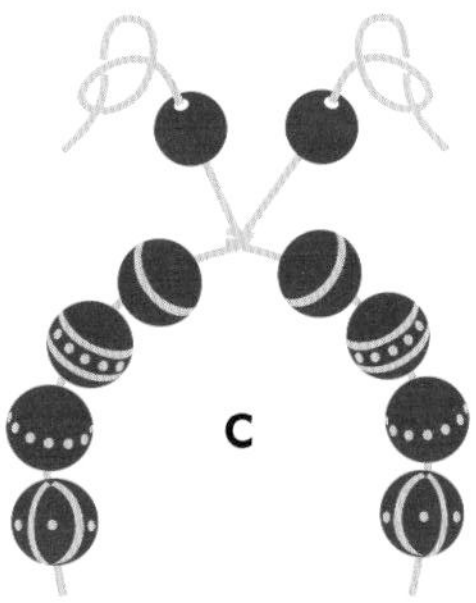

C

4 Halve the elasticated thread for either a necklace or a bracelet. Thread on the beads, alternating the designs. To finish off, tie the ends in a double knot. Decorate the thread ends with small beads secured with a double knot.

Pretty Flower Earrings **

Materials required
SET OF EARRINGS
- *2 earring mounts and backing, 2cm (3/4in) in diameter*
- *a fine needle*
- *white thread*
- *faceted beads in orange, 10 for each earring*
- *small round beads in iridescent turquoise blue, 69 for each earring*
- *small glass beads in lime green, 72 for each earring*
- *flat-nosed pliers*

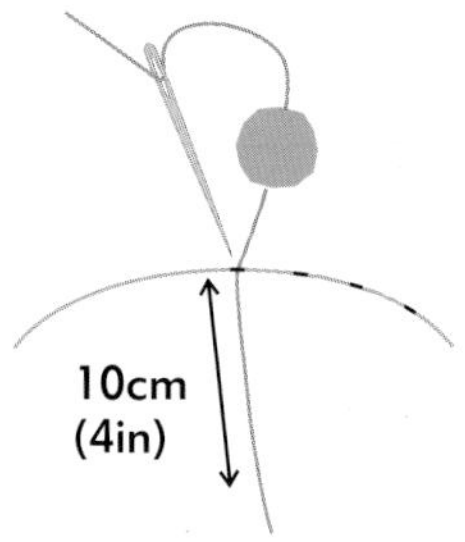
10cm
(4in)

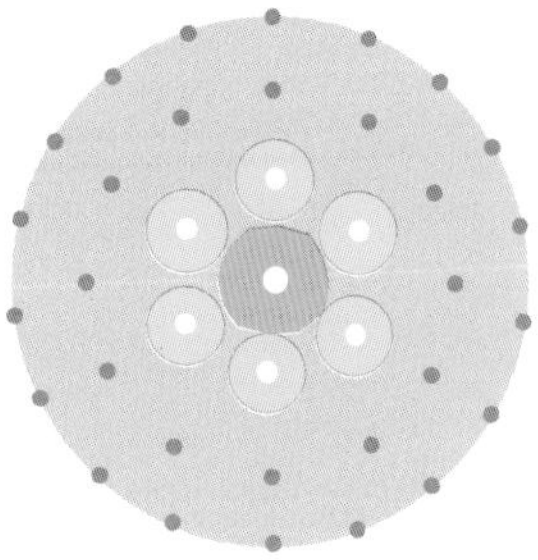

Instructions are given for making one earring. Repeat the process to make a pair of earrings.

1 Thread the needle with 50cm (20in) white thread. Bring through from the wrong side of the earring mount at the centre. Leave 10cm (4in) of thread on the reverse. Thread on an orange faceted bead and take the needle back through the same hole.

2 Bring the needle through from the wrong side on the second row of the mount. Thread on a turquoise bead and take the needle back through the next hole. Come up at the next hole, thread on another turquoise bead and go back through the next hole. Work around the second row in this way.

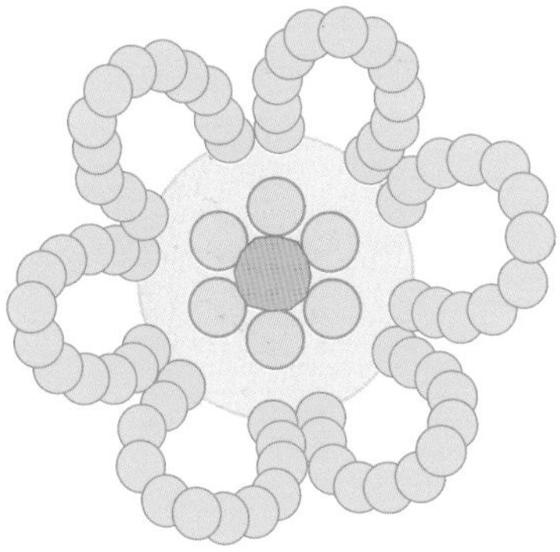

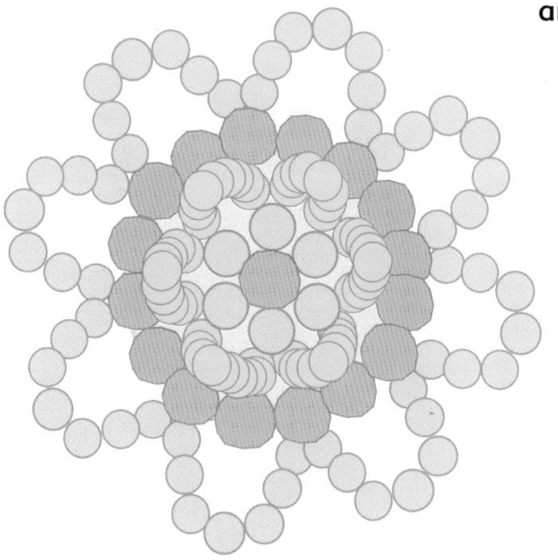

3 Come up at a hole on the third row and thread on 12 green beads to make a petal, then go back into the next hole. Come up at the following hole, thread on another 12 green beads and so on. Ensure that you never enter the same hole more than once.

4 Take the needle through from the right side to the wrong side on the last row of the backing. Thread on an orange faceted bead and go back in through the next hole. Continue as in step 2. To make the last ring of petals, come through to the right side and thread on 7 turquoise beads. Work as you did in step 3. Finish on the wrong side and tie a knot with the two threads. Trim excess thread.

5 Place the backing on the mount and secure with the flat-nosed pliers, taking care not to damage the beads.

Butterflies in Flight **

Materials required

BUTTERFLY

- *25cm (10in) wire 0.7mm ($^1/_{32}$in) in diameter*
- *2.3m (7ft 7in) stainless steel wire 0.3mm ($^1/_{64}$in) in diameter*
- *small glass beads in assorted colours*
- *flat-nosed pliers*
- *hairclip or wooden hairpin*
- *metal glue*

Use these small butterflies as decorations for the home or to make pretty brooches.

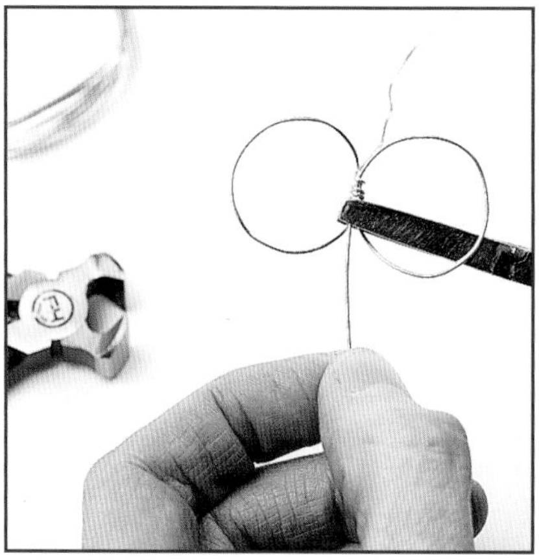

1 For the butterfly shape, make a figure of eight shape with the 25cm (10in) length of wire and secure in the middle with four twists of wire. Flatten out the body of the butterfly using the flat-nosed pliers and trim the excess wire.

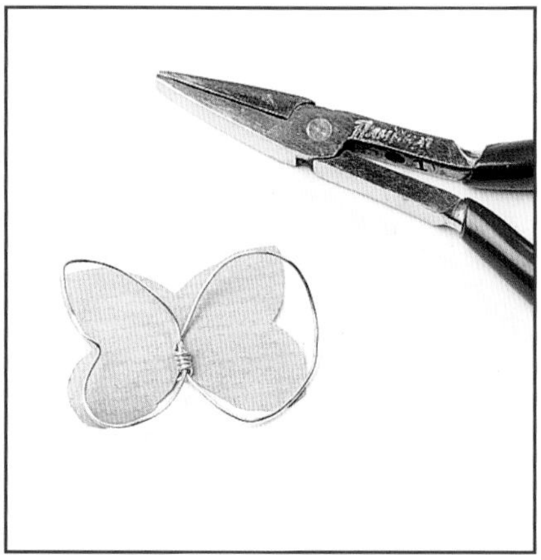

2 Trace off the butterfly template (see page 109) and place the wire figure of eight on top of it. Shape the wire to the butterfly shape using pliers.

3 Take a 1.2m (4ft) length of stainless steel wire and wind it three times around one of the butterfly wings. Thread on a bead, pull it tight, and wind the wire tightly around the base wire three times. Work in this way around the body and two wings.

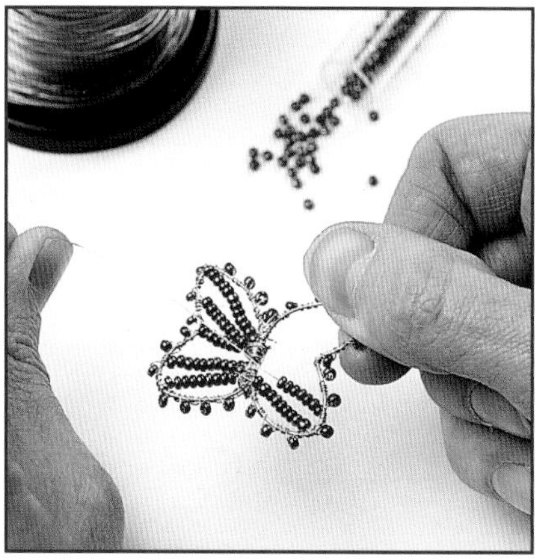

4 To work the inside of the wings, take a 1m (39in) length of stainless steel wire and knot one of the ends on to one of the butterfly wings. Thread on a string of beads and wind the wire three times around the opposite point on the centre body. Make five strands on each butterfly wing.

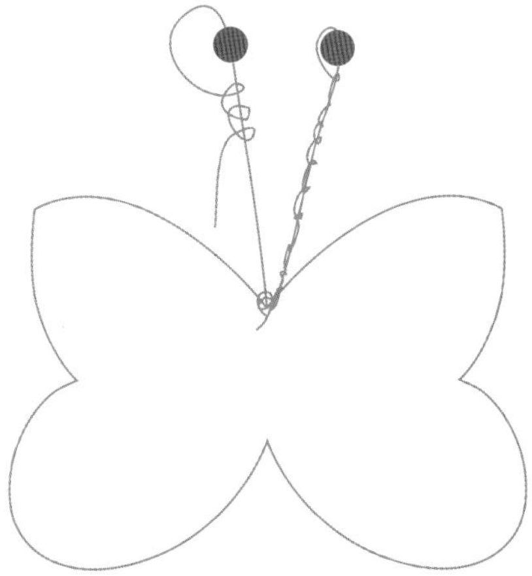

5 To create the antennae, wind the centre of an 8cm ($3^1/_8$in) length of stainless steel wire between the two wings (see diagram above). Position a bead on each wire, 2cm ($^3/_4$in) from the butterfly, then bend the wire back over the top of the bead, and wind it around itself. Glue the butterfly to the hairclip.

Sequined Flower Choker ★★

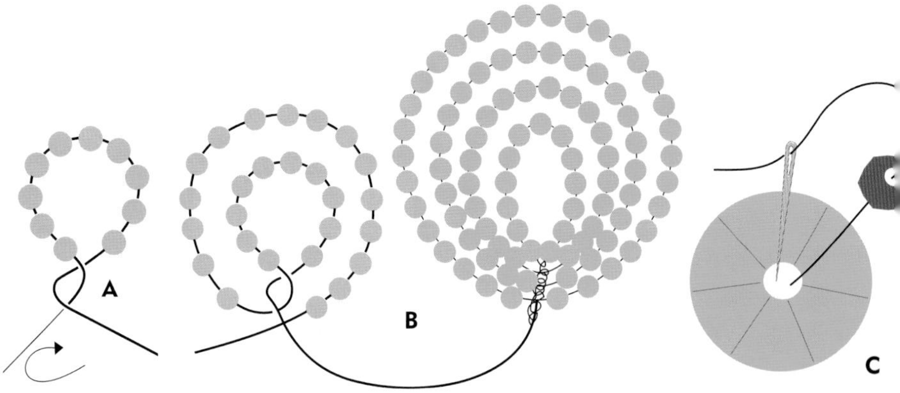
A
B
C

Materials required

MAUVE CHOKER

- *small glass beads in pink and mauve*
- *2 x 37cm ($14^{1}/_{2}$in) rows of stitched sequins in pale pink*
- *89cm (35in) of 1.5cm ($^{5}/_{8}$in) wide satin ribbon in mauve*
- *needle, mauve thread, thin wire*
- *1 large sequin in pink or pale pink*
- *1 large faceted bead in mauve*

MAROON CHOKER

- *small glass beads in deep iridescent maroon*
- *89cm (35in) of 1cm ($^{3}/_{8}$in) wide satin ribbon in maroon*
- *37cm ($14^{1}/_{2}$in) stitched sequins in maroon*
- *needle, black thread, thin wire*
- *large pink sequin*
- *large iridescent pink bead*

To make a bracelet: make up the flower using small glass beads in pink, a sequin and a faceted bead in mauve. To make the wrist strap, sew 17cm ($6^{3}/_{4}$in) maroon stitched sequins and 17cm ($6^{3}/_{4}$in) pale pink stitched sequins on to a 46cm (18in) lavender blue ribbon.

To make the flower

❶ To create a petal, cut a 1m (39in) length of thin wire. Thread on 10 small glass beads 2cm ($^{3}/_{4}$in) from the end, then make a loop. Close the loop by turning it once on itself to twist the wire (see diagram A). Make a second circle by threading on around 20 beads and winding it around itself again to secure. Work in this way for two more circles, threading on 25 and then 35 beads.

❷ Make up a further four petals in the same way, leaving a 2cm ($^{3}/_{4}$in) length of wire between each petal (see diagram B). Turn the remaining wire around on itself several times to tighten all the petals. Trim the excess wire.

To make the choker

❶ For the mauve choker make up two rows with pink beads and two with mauve beads for each of the five petals. Use all maroon beads for the maroon choker.

❷ For the mauve choker use mauve thread and sew two rows of stitched sequins on to the ribbon, positioning them so the ends of the ribbon are undecorated and can be tied in a fastening. Stitch over the threads linking the sequins together, and sew a small glass bead on the final sequin to secure. For the maroon choker use black thread and secure a single row of stitched sequins.

❸ Position the flowers at the centre of the choker, with a large sequin on top of the centre of the flower. Bring a needle and thread through from the wrong side and thread on the large faceted bead, then take the needle back through the sequin and secure the flower on the wrong side of the choker.

Beaded Flower Motifs ★★

Materials required

BEAD MOTIF
- *small glass beads in dark orange, deep pink, bronze or gold*
- *25cm (10in) square of cotton fabric in khaki, fuchsia or rusty red*
- *pink, gold, orange or bronze thread*
- *white dressmaker's pencil*
- *embroidery hoop*
- *a fine needle*

BROOCH
- *5cm (2in) square of thin card*
- *stick-on brooch mount*

BELT
- *2.5cm (1in) wide suede strip*
- *strip of Velcro*

NECKLACE
- *small glass beads in orange and gold*
- *thread*

A

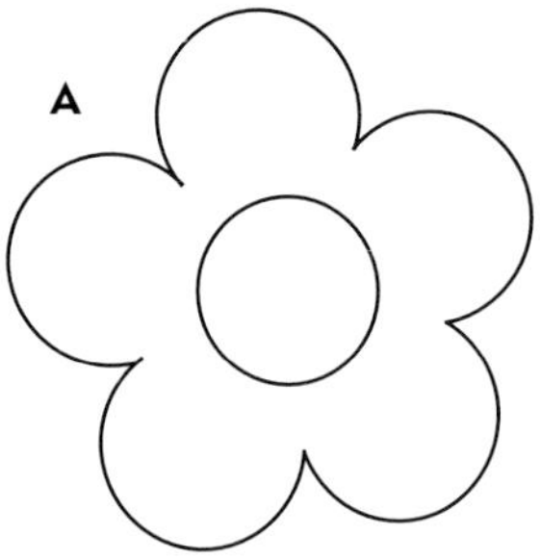

B

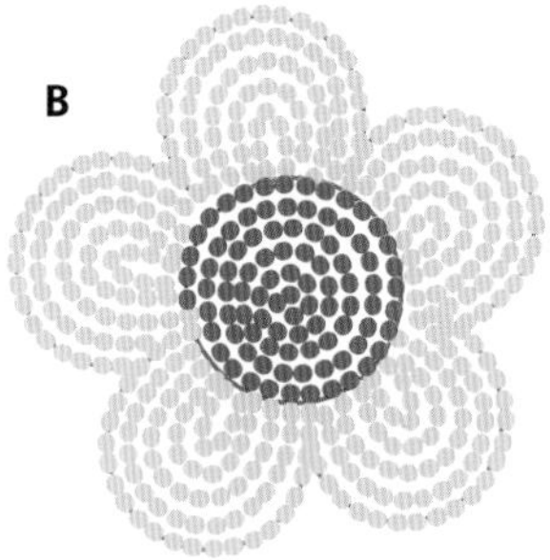

To make the bead motif

❶ Trace off flower motif (A) and transfer to the centre of the fabric using white dressmaker's pencil.

❷ Centre the motif in the embroidery hoop, keeping the fabric tight. Stitch the beads around the outer edge of the centre flower circle and work in concentric circles towards the centre. Sew on a central bead, then sew a back stitch so that you return to the outside edge of the flower centre.

❸ Using different coloured beads embroider the petals: start from the centre of each petal and work outwards. If necessary, fill in any empty spaces with additional beads.

To make the brooch

❶ Cut the fabric with the flower motif down to a 15cm (6in) square. Cut four 5.5cm (2 1/8in) squares from each corner (see diagram C, page 108).

❷ Centre the square card beneath the motif. Fold the four flaps to the back and glue in place. Keep the fabric taut and cut any excess for a perfect finish.

❸ Glue on the brooch mount 1cm (3/8in) from the upper edge of the flower motif.

To make the belt

Mount the flower motif on to cardboard as for the brooch (see steps 1 and 2), then glue it in the centre of the suede strip. Cut the belt to the required length and glue Velcro in place to make a fastening.

To make the necklace

Cut out a 12 x 7cm (4 3/4 x 2 3/4in) rectangle around the flower (see diagram D, page 108). Fold the rectangle in half widthways, enclosing the flower (you end up with a rectangle 6 x 7 cm (2 3/8 x 2 3/4in)). Sew two sides together 1cm (3/8in) from the edges (see diagram E, page 108). Turn the pocket inside out. Fold the upper edges 1cm (3/8in) over towards the inside of the pocket and iron. Make a 60cm (24in) neck strap with orange and gold beads. Sew each end on to either side of the pocket.

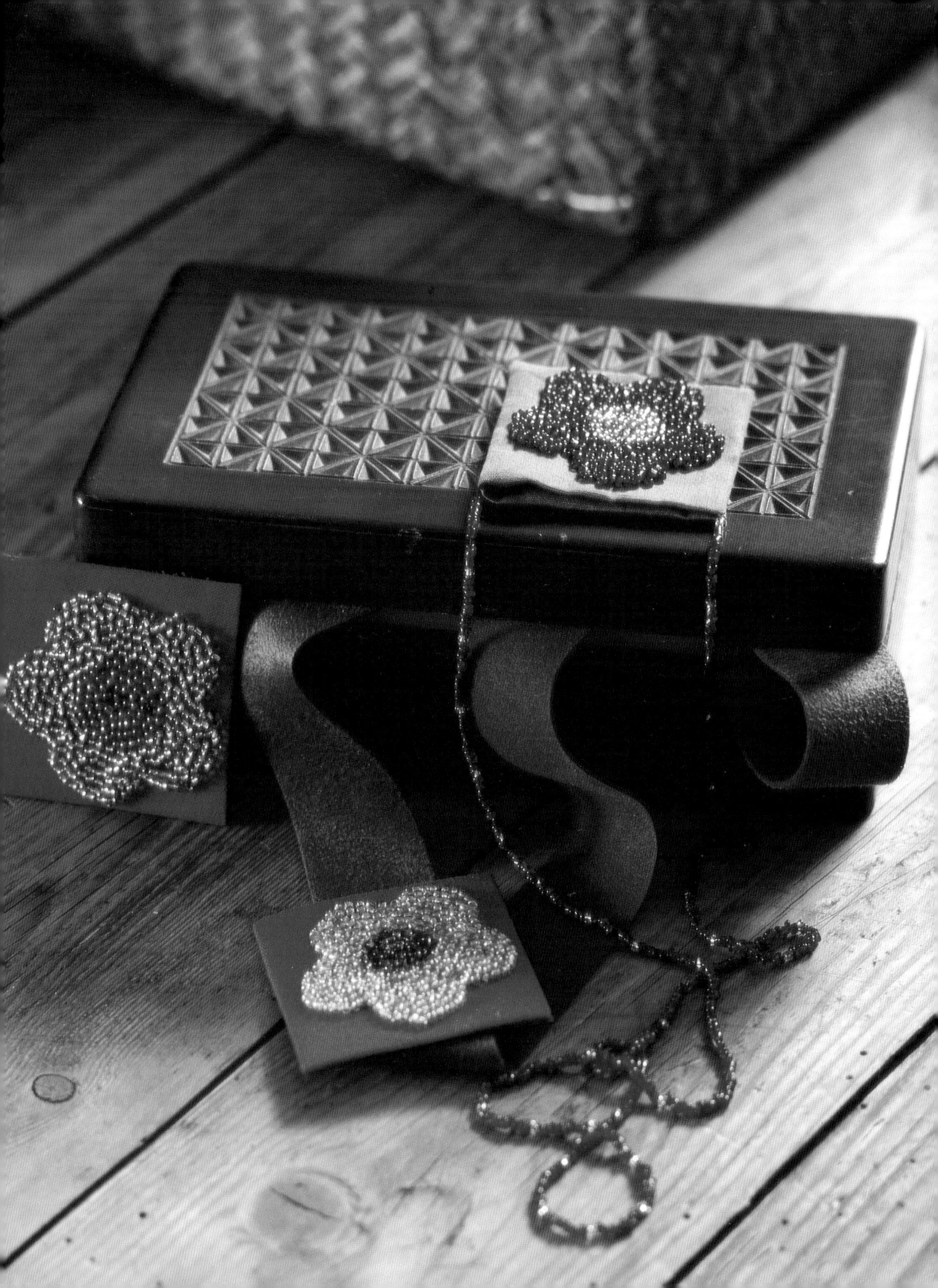

Silk Flowers ★★★

Materials required

PALE PINK FLOWER

- *pink enamelled wire*
- *satin and satin ribbon in pale pink*
- *fabric glue*
- *80 small glass beads in pink*
- *80 small glass beads in orange*
- *15 crimp beads*
- *5 large round beads in pink*
- *65 faceted beads in pink*
- *5 large sequins in pink*
- *20 small sequins in orange*
- *safety pin*
- *flat-nosed pliers*

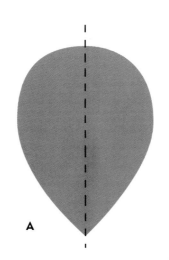

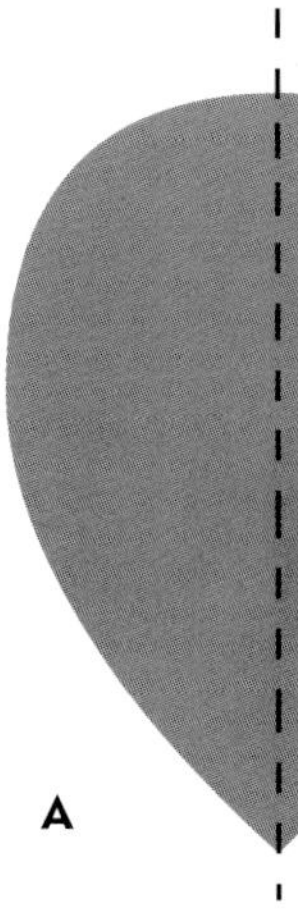

A

❶ To make the petals:

Cut seventeen 12cm (4$\frac{3}{4}$in) lengths of wire. Trace around the petal template (see diagram above) and cut out 11 satin petals. Fold along the central vein of each petal, position a length of wire over the bottom two thirds and glue in place (see diagrams B and C, page 109). Fold the petal in half carefully and use your nail to crease the fold in the vein. Trace around the large petal template (see diagram D, page 109) and make up in the same way.

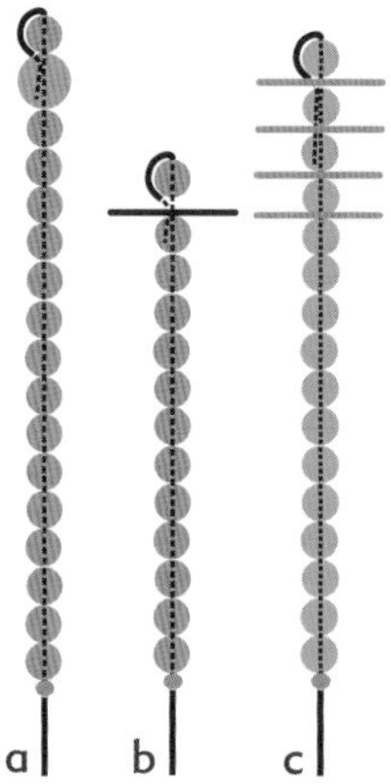
a
b
c

E

❷ To make the stamens:

Cut fifteen 12cm (4$\frac{3}{4}$in) lengths of pink wire. Make up 5 stamens following diagram E(a) as a guide. Thread one small glass bead nearly to the end of the wire, then fold the wire back over the bead and slide a large bead over both wires. Thread on the remaining beads. Finish with a crimp bead and squeeze it flat with flat-nosed pliers. Make up 5 more stamens using faceted beads and diagram E(b) as a guide and 5 others following diagram E(c). Intersperse small sequins as shown and finish off each time with a crimp bead.

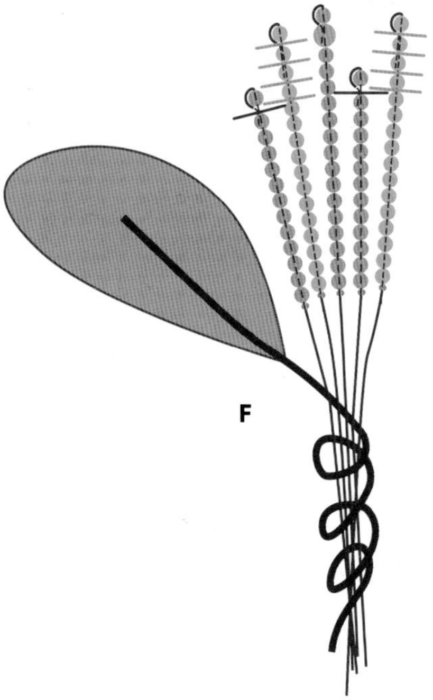

F

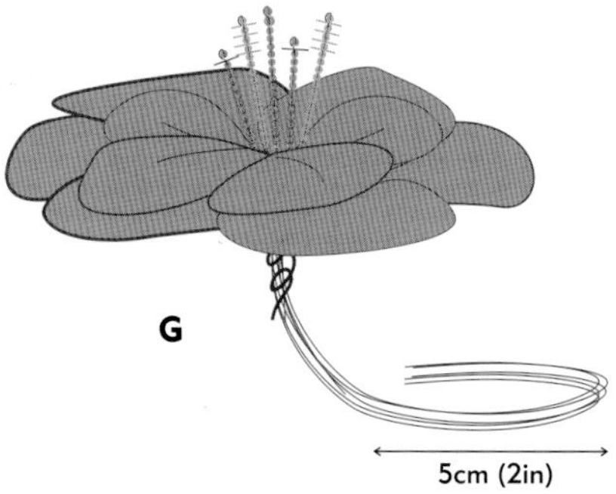
5cm (2in)

G

❸ Combine the stamens and attach the smaller petals by winding the wires around the stamens (see diagram F). Attach the larger petals in the same way.

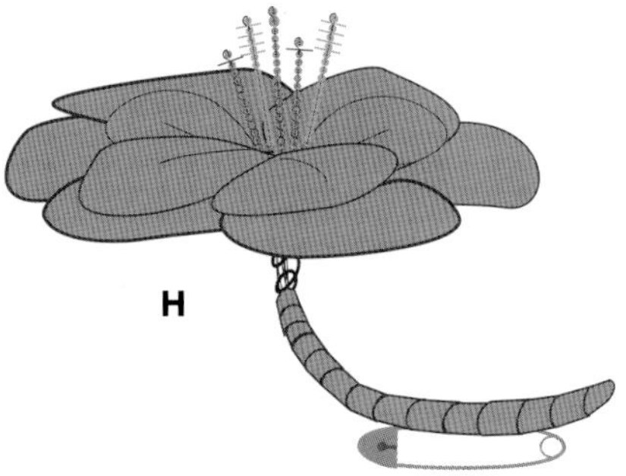

H

❹ Bend the wires back on themselves to give a length of 5cm (2in) (see diagram G). Halve the satin ribbon lengthways and wrap it around the wires. Secure the ends with a little glue. Attach the safety pin to the stem to make a brooch (diagram H).

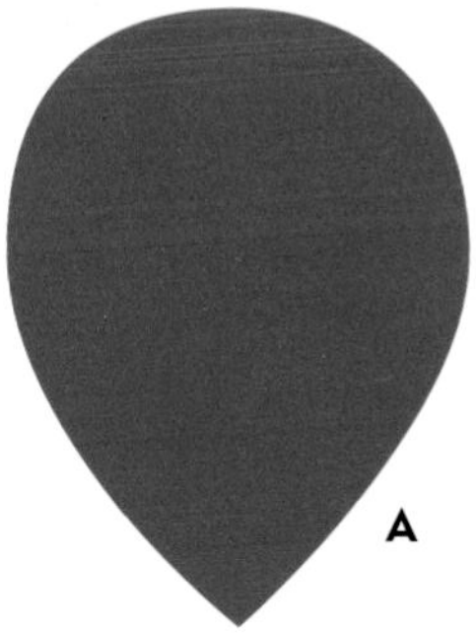
A

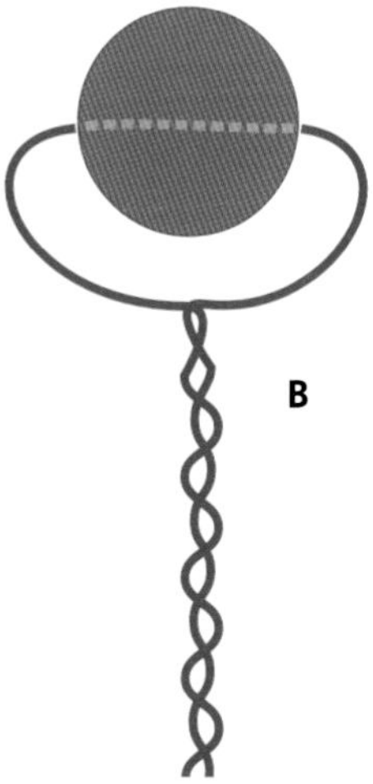
B

Materials required

FUCHSIA FLOWER

- *pink enamelled wire*
- *satin and satin ribbon in fuchsia pink*
- *fabric glue*
- *5 faceted beads in purple*
- *5 faceted beads in mauve*
- *5 faceted beads in vivid pink*
- *20 crimp beads*
- *5 sequins in pink*
- *safety pin*

❶ Cut forty 12cm ($4^{3}/_{4}$in) lengths of wire. Trace around the petal template above (diagram A) and cut 20 petals out of the satin. Attach them to 20 lengths of wire as for the pale pink flower (see page 66, step 1).

❷ Thread a bead or sequin on to the remaining lengths of wire. Bend each wire into two equal lengths and twist them together tightly to secure the bead or sequin (see diagram B). Assemble the stamens and petals as for the pink flower (see page 66, steps 2, 3 and 4).

Materials required

LAVENDER BLUE FLOWER

- *blue enamelled wire*
- *satin and satin ribbon in lavender blue*
- *fabric glue*
- *55 small glass beads in mauve*
- *20 faceted beads in mauve*
- *35 faceted beads in purple*
- *5 large faceted beads in purple*
- *10 crimp beads*
- *5 sequins in purple*
- *safety pin*

Cut twenty-five 12 cm (4$^{3}/_{4}$in) lengths of wire. Trace around the template opposite and cut 10 petals out of the satin. Using purple sequins, make up five stamens following the same technique as for the Fuchsia Flower (see page 68, step 2). Make up another 10 stamens following the same technique as for the Pink Flower (see page 66, step 2) and using the beads of your choice. Assemble as for the Pink Flower.

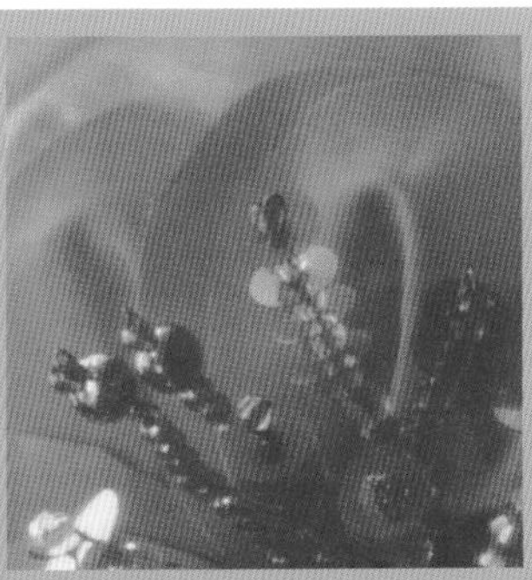

Festive Decorations ★★

Materials required

SQUARE DECORATION

- *pieces of felt in red, 5 x 15cm (2 x 6in); pink 12 x 8.5cm ($4^3/_4$ x $3^3/_8$in); and purple, 5 x 10cm (2 x 4in)*
- *silver beads and bugles*
- *silver sequins*
- *perforated stars*
- *small glass beads in pink*
- *a fine needle*
- *thin card*

To make heart-shaped decorations, trace off the template on page 109 and transfer to thin card. Use as a guide for cutting out the pieces of felt.

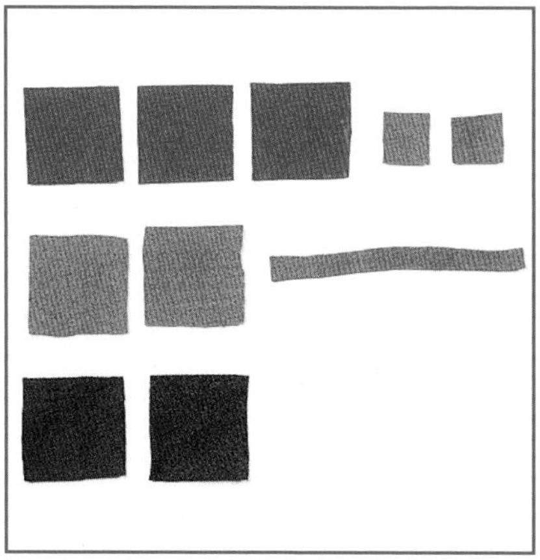

1 Cut out three red, two pink and two purple 5cm (2in) felt squares. Cut out two pink 2.5cm (1in) felt squares and a pink felt strip 12 x 1cm ($4^3/_4$ x $^3/_8$in), which will act as the handle.

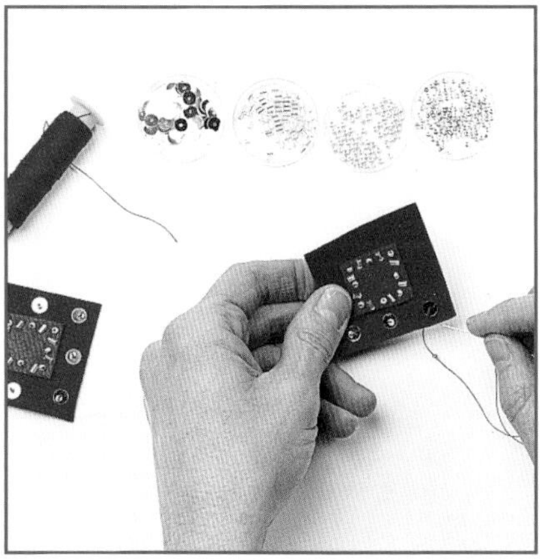

2 Place a small square in the centre of one of the large squares and, using a fine needle, sew on silver beads and bugles around the inner edge of the small square. Sew on sequins around the edge of the large square, securing each one with a bead (see page 74, diagram E). Prepare two decorated squares in this way.

3 Decorate the felt strip with sequins secured with beads and attach it to an undecorated large pink square to make a little handle.

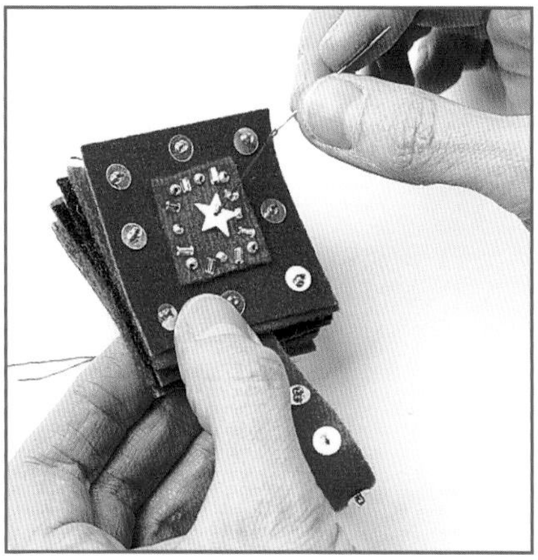

4 Stack seven different coloured squares together, placing the decorated square on top and the square with the handle at the centre. Bring a needle and thread through the centre of the decorated square from the wrong side, thread on a star and a small glass bead then go back through the hole in the star and through the seven squares. Attach another star and bead on the last square to hold the squares together. Finish with a small stitch on the reverse of the last square.

Why not vary your decorations by using your favourite colour combinations? Try using this idea to create key ring decorations or to make fancy curtain tiebacks.

Beaded Suede Jewellery ⋆

Materials required

- *suede ribbon in maroon, khaki green or beige: 20cm (8in) of 1.5cm (5/8in) wide ribbon for a bracelet, 40cm (16in) of 1cm (3/8in) wide ribbon for a necklace, 45cm (18in) of 2.5cm (1in) wide ribbon for a headband*
- *leather and suede punch*
- *small glass beads in assorted shapes and colours to match the ribbon*
- *4 large beads*
- *black felt-tip pen*
- *ruler*
- *thread*
- *a needle*
- *25cm (10in) thick elastic*
- *fabric glue*

1 For the bracelet: On the reverse of the suede ribbon, use the felt-tip pen to mark the position of the holes using the measurements indicated in the diagram below.

Bracelet

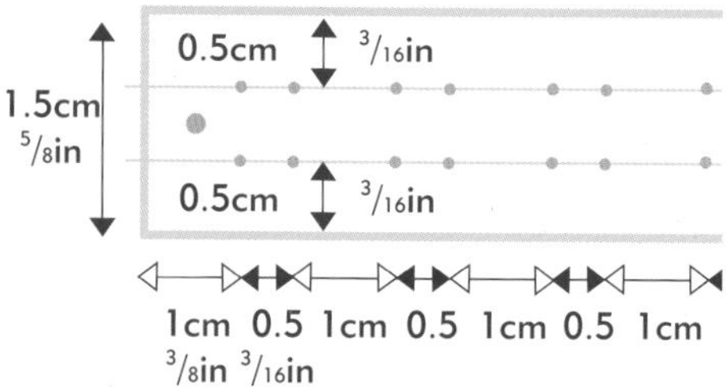

0.5cm 3/16in
1.5cm 5/8in
0.5cm 3/16in
1cm 0.5 1cm 0.5 1cm 0.5 1cm
3/8in 3/16in

2 For the necklace: On the reverse of the suede ribbon, use the felt-tip pen to mark the position of the holes using the measurements indicated in the diagram below.

Necklace

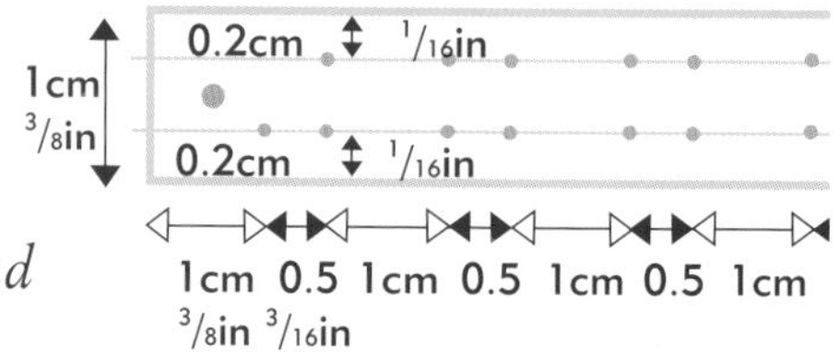

0.2cm 1/16in
1cm 3/8in
0.2cm 1/16in
1cm 0.5 1cm 0.5 1cm 0.5 1cm
3/8in 3/16in

3 For the headband: On the reverse of the suede ribbon, use the felt-tip pen to mark the position of the holes using the measurements indicated in the diagram below.

Headband

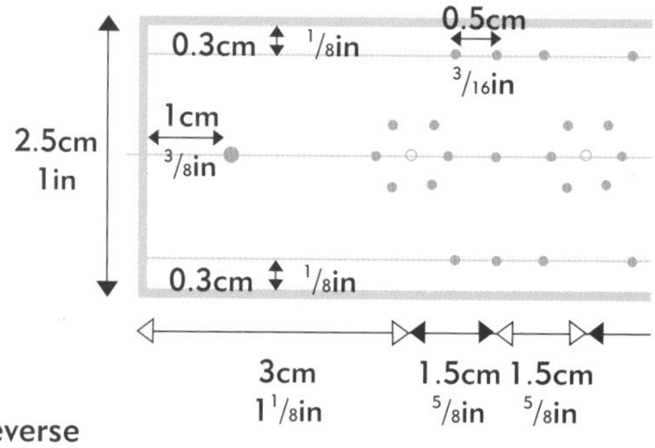

0.3cm 1/8in
0.5cm 3/16in
1cm 3/8in
2.5cm 1in
0.3cm 1/8in
3cm 1 1/8in
1.5cm 1.5cm
5/8in 5/8in

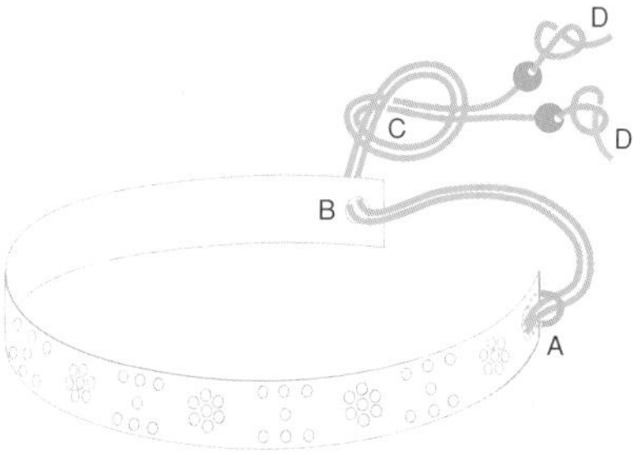

D
C
D
B
A

4 To pierce the ribbon: Set the punch to the second hole size. Place it over the felt-tip marks and press to pierce.

5 To decorate and fasten: Decorate the bracelet and necklace with small glass beads. Go through each bead twice with your needle and thread to secure, starting from the reverse of the fabric. Make a fastening by piercing one end of the suede ribbon and sewing a large bead on the other end.

Decorate the headband with beads and/or the suede lozenges that fall out of the punch. To make a fastening, make a hole 1cm (3/8in) from each end. Halve the elastic and thread the loop into hole A, then both ends of elastic into hole B. Tie a knot (C) and decorate the ends with beads (see diagram left).

Sequined Grosgrain Jewellery

Materials required

- *75cm (29 1/2in) grosgrain ribbon to make one necklace and 40cm (16in) to make one bracelet*
- *dressmaker's pencil*
- *2 types of perforated sequins*
- *3 types of bugles*
- *3 types of small glass beads*
- *thread to match the ribbon*
- *a needle*
- *glue*
- *1 small button*

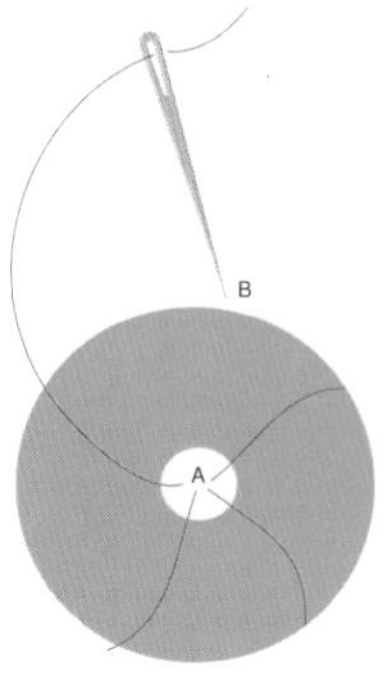
B
A

C *Sequin sewn on with star motif*

D *Row of couched beads*

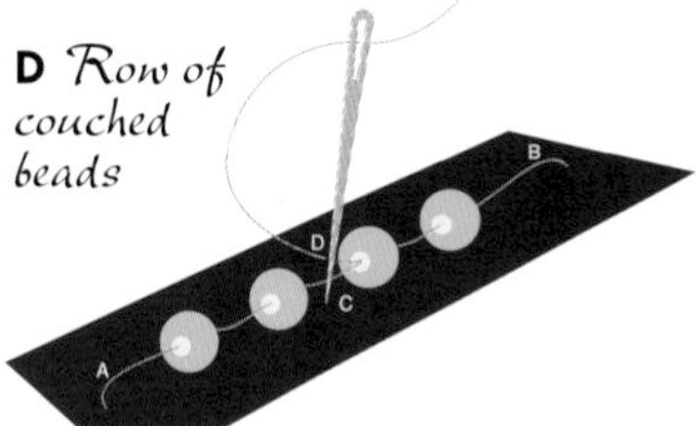
B
D
C
A

A *Starting off*

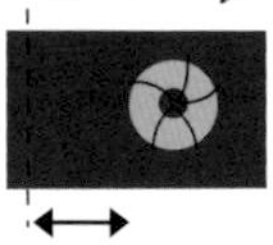
1cm
(3/8in)

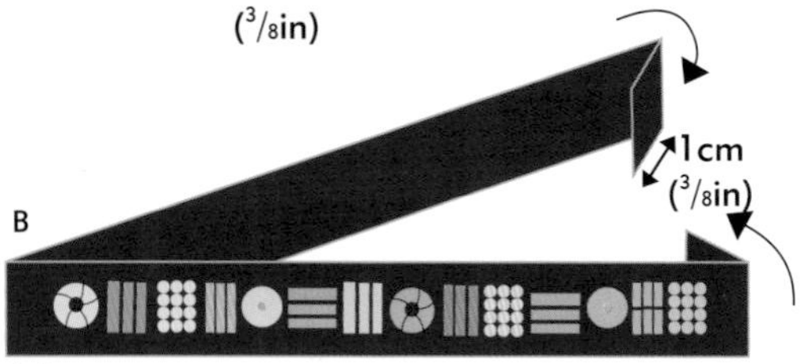
B
1cm
(3/8in)
1cm
(3/8in)

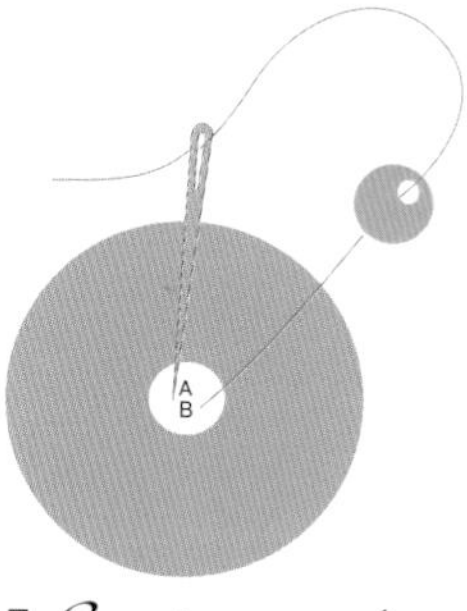
A
B

E *Sequin secured with bead*

1 Use the dressmaker's pencil to mark the lengthways central point on the grosgrain ribbon. Starting 1cm (3/8in) from this mark sew on the beads in a straight line (see diagram A).

2 Using diagram B as a guide, alternate between a perforated sequin sewn on with a star motif (see diagram C), three rows of vertical bugles, three rows of four vertical couched beads (see diagram D), three rows of vertical bugles, one sequin held in place by a bead (see diagram E), three rows of horizontal bugles and three rows of vertical bugles. Continue to work in this way, finishing the final motif 2cm (3/4in) from the right-hand edge of the ribbon.

3 Fold in a 1cm (3/8in) flap at each end of the ribbon (see diagram B) and glue down. Then glue the beaded section of the ribbon to the non-beaded section. Sew on the small button at one end of the ribbon; at the other end make a loop (see diagram F) the size of the button with three strands of thread and go over the loop with a buttonhole stitch (see page 15).

You can make these pieces of jewellery using other types of ribbon such as velvet.

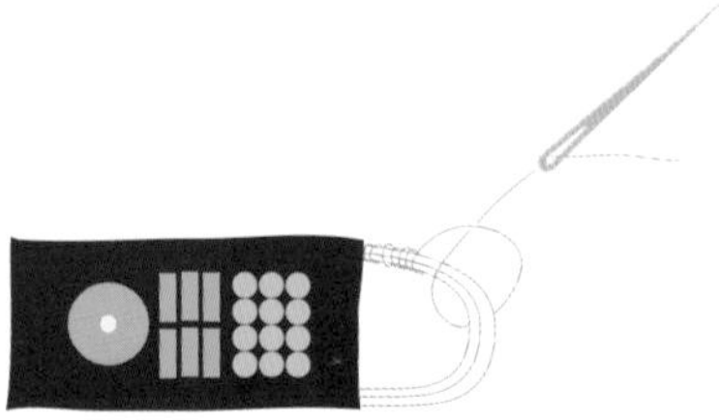

F *Loop*

You could use a small piece of rat-tail cord in place of the button loop.

Sparkly Felt Designs ★★

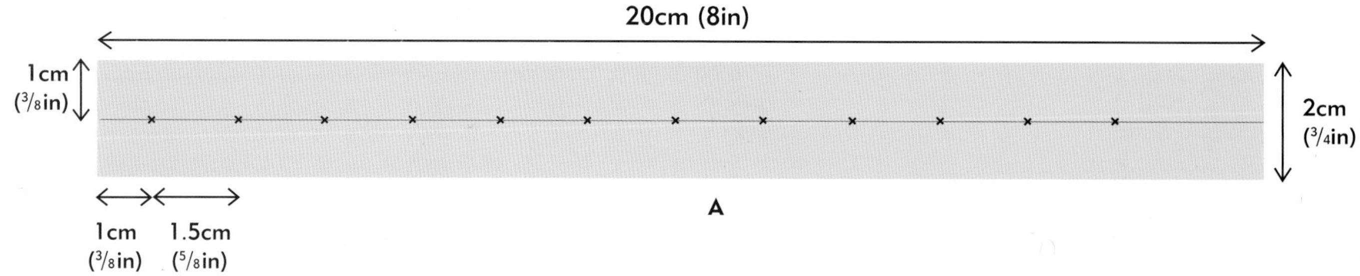
20cm (8in)
1cm (3/8in)
2cm (3/4in)
1cm (3/8in)
1.5cm (5/8in)
A

Materials required

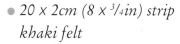

BRACELET

- *20 x 2cm (8 x 3/4in) strip khaki felt*
- *black felt-tip pen*
- *a fine needle*
- *khaki thread*
- *6 large flat sequins in silver*
- *12 small faceted beads in turquoise*
- *roughly 85 small round beads in turquoise*
- *roughly 42 small beads in silver*
- *20 x 2cm (8 x 3/4in) strip turquoise felt*
- *fabric glue*
- *1 press-stud*

1. Using the felt-tip pen, draw a horizontal line on the reverse of the strip of khaki felt dividing the fabric in half lengthways. Make a mark 1cm (3/8in) from one of the ends and then at 1.5cm (5/8in) intervals. Stop 2.5cm (1in) from the other end (see diagram A).

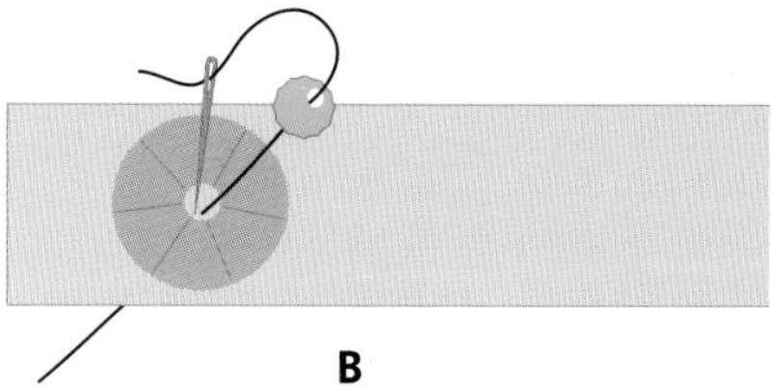
B

2. Bring a needle and thread through the first mark from the wrong side of the fabric. Thread on a large silver sequin and a faceted bead and go back through the sequin (see diagram B). Sew small round beads tightly around the outside of the sequin (see diagram C).

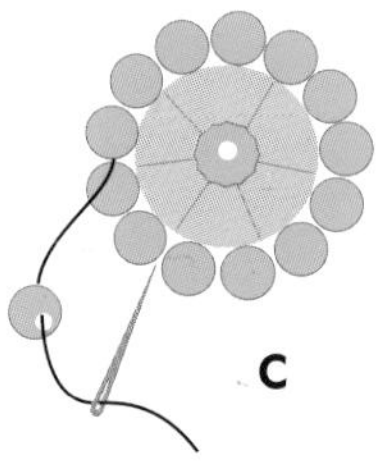
C

3. Bring a needle and thread through the second mark from the wrong side of the fabric. Thread on a faceted bead and go back through to the other side of the fabric. Sew small silver beads around the faceted bead (see diagram D). Alternate these two designs until you reach the final mark on the felt.

D

4. Glue the decorated strip to the turquoise strip using fabric glue. Leave to dry for three hours before sewing on the press-stud 0.6cm (1/4in) from the ends to fasten.

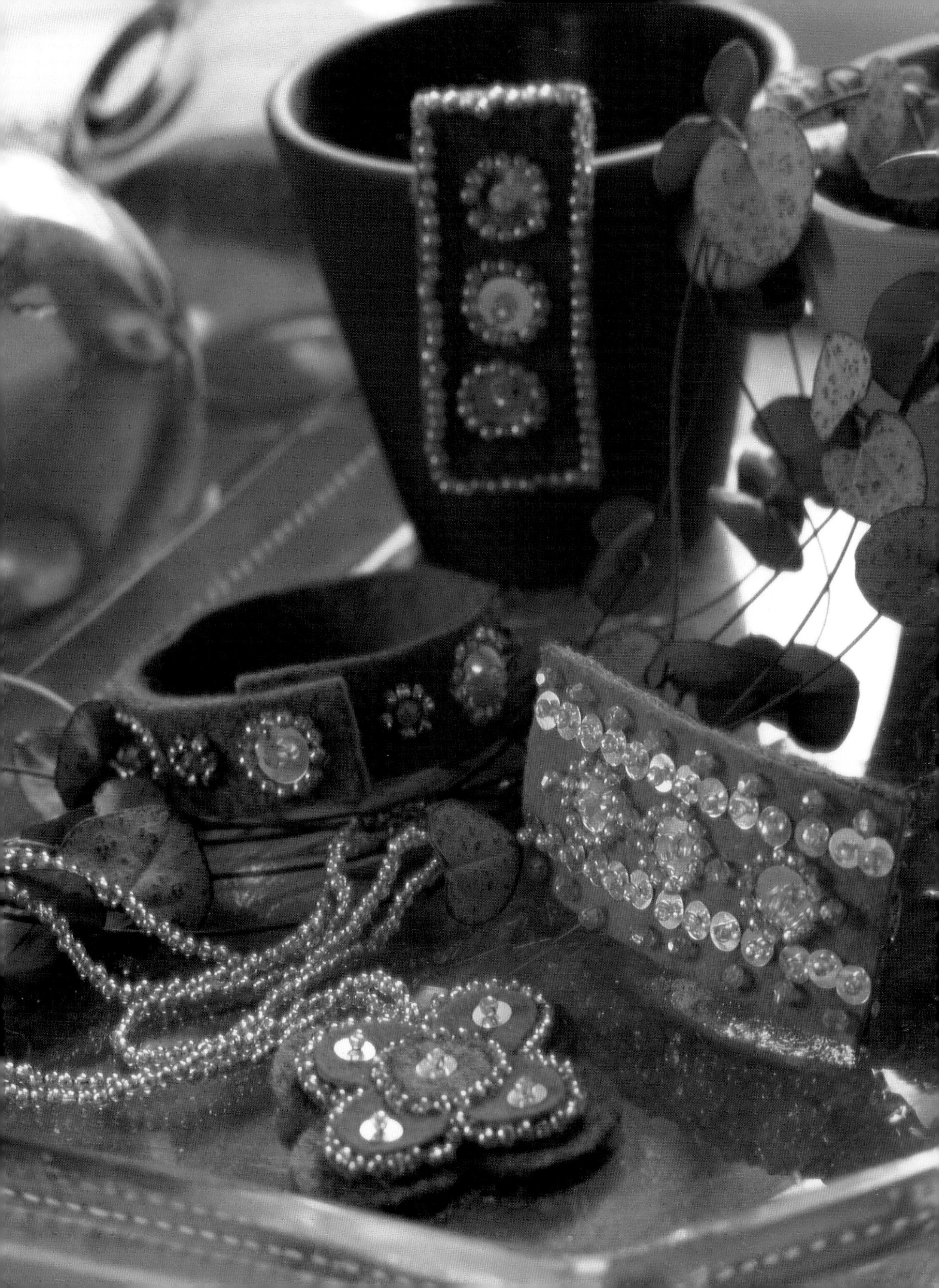

Materials required

KHAKI HAIRCLIP

- *7 x 3cm ($2\frac{3}{4}$ x $1\frac{1}{4}$in) strip felt in khaki*
- *black felt-tip pen*
- *a fine needle, khaki thread*
- *3 large sequins in silver*
- *3 small faceted beads in turquoise*
- *roughly 110 small round beads in turquoise*
- *7 x 3cm ($2\frac{3}{4}$ x $1\frac{1}{4}$in) strip felt in turquoise*
- *fabric glue and jewellery glue*
- *6cm ($2\frac{3}{8}$in) hairclip*

TURQUOISE HAIRCLIP

- *8 x 4cm ($3\frac{1}{8}$ x $1\frac{5}{8}$in) strip felt in turquoise*
- *black felt-tip pen*
- *roughly 25 small faceted beads in turquoise*
- *roughly 26 small sequins in silver*
- *roughly 65 small round beads in turquoise*
- *3 large sequins in silver*
- *8 x 4cm ($3\frac{1}{8}$ x $1\frac{5}{8}$in) strip felt in khaki*
- *fine needle*
- *thread*
- *fabric glue and jewellery glue*
- *8cm ($3\frac{1}{8}$in) hairclip*

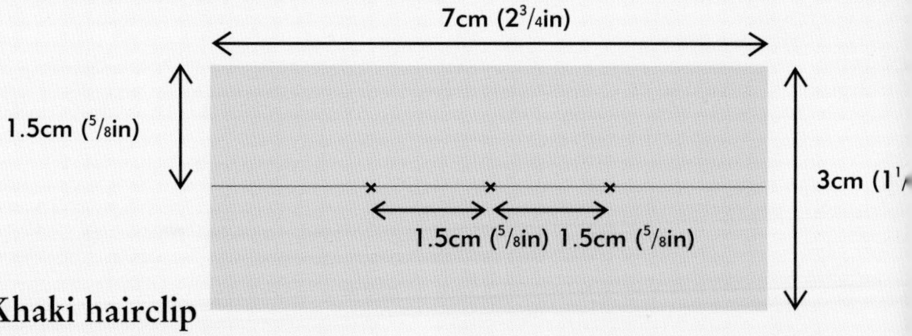
7cm (2³/4in)
1.5cm (⁵/8in)
3cm (1¹/
1.5cm (⁵/8in) 1.5cm (⁵/8in)

Khaki hairclip

1 Draw a horizontal line on the felt, dividing it in half lengthways (see diagram above). Mark a point 2cm ($\frac{3}{4}$in) from one of the ends, then two more at 1.5cm ($\frac{5}{8}$in) intervals. Sew a silver sequin secured by a faceted bead at each mark (see diagram B, page 76).

2 Sew small round turquoise beads close together along the edges of the khaki strip. Glue the decorated strip of felt on to the turquoise strip with fabric glue, then glue to the hairclip using jewellery glue.

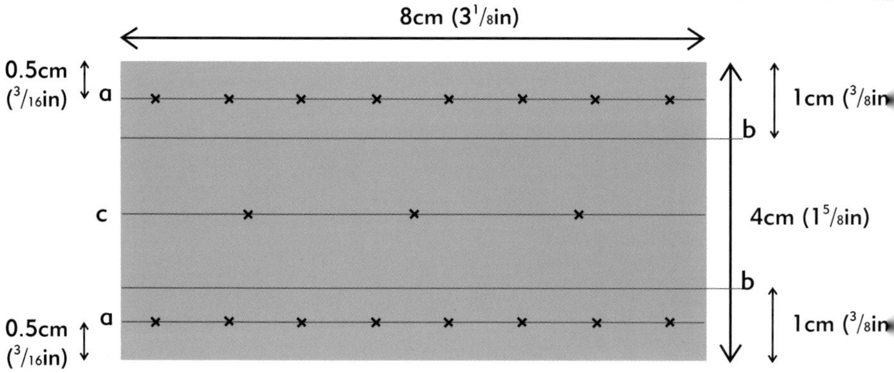
8cm (3¹/8in)
0.5cm (³/16in)
a
1cm (³/8in
b
c
4cm (1⁵/8in)
b
a
0.5cm (³/16in)
1cm (³/8in

A

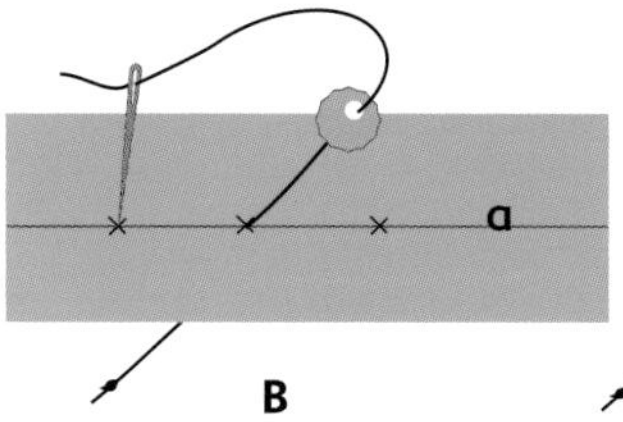
a

B

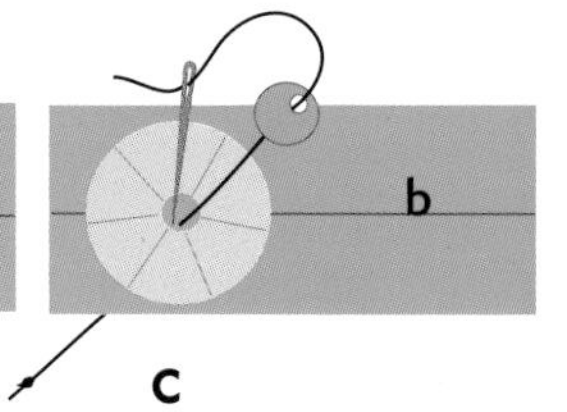
b

C

Turquoise hairclip

1 Mark guidelines in felt-tip on the turquoise felt (see diagram A).
Lines a: draw two horizontal lines 0.5cm ($\frac{3}{16}$in) from the upper and lower edge of the fabric. Make a mark 0.5cm ($\frac{3}{16}$in) from one end, then seven more at 1cm ($\frac{3}{8}$in) intervals.
Lines b: draw two horizontal lines 1cm ($\frac{3}{8}$in) from the upper and lower edges of the strip.
Line c: draw a horizontal line 2cm ($\frac{3}{4}$in) from the upper edge of the fabric. Make a mark 2cm ($\frac{3}{4}$in) from one end and then two more at 2cm ($\frac{3}{4}$in) intervals.

2 Sew a faceted bead at each mark along lines a (see diagram B). Sew small silver sequins close together along lines b, securing each one with a small round turquoise bead (see diagram C). Sew a large silver sequin surrounded by round turquoise beads at each mark on line c (see diagram C, page 76), then sew a turquoise faceted bead either side of each motif.

3 Glue the decorated felt to the khaki strip with fabric glue, then to the hairclip with jewellery glue.

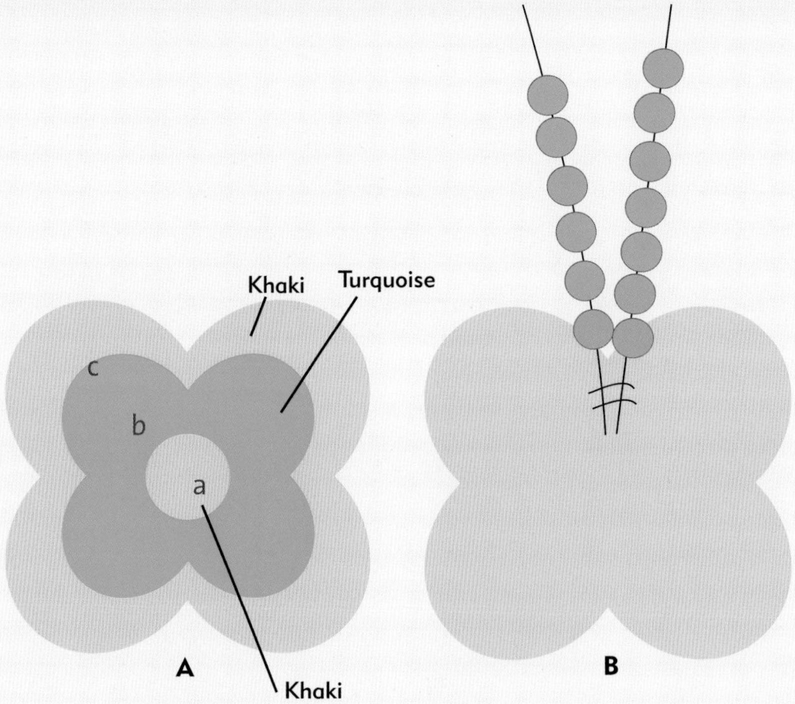
Khaki
Turquoise
c
b
a
A
Khaki
B

❶ Trace off the flower template above (see diagram A) and cut out of the felt squares.

❷ Using khaki thread, sew a silver sequin in the centre of each petal of the turquoise flower (b) and secure with a bead (see page 76, diagram C). Repeat in the centre of the flower circle (a).

❸ Thread the small turquoise beads on to the wire. Sew the two ends of wire between two petals of the large khaki flower (diagram B).

❹ Assemble the felt petals: glue the khaki centre on the turquoise flower, then glue the turquoise flower on the large khaki flower. Sew a row of turquoise beads around the edge of the khaki centre and the turquoise flower.

Materials required

PENDANT

- *2 x 13cm (5 1/8in) squares of khaki felt*
- *5cm (2in) square of turquoise felt*
- *black felt-tip pen*
- *fine needle, turquoise thread*
- *5 small sequins in silver*
- *small round beads in turquoise*
- *70cm (27 1/2in) wire*
- *fabric glue*

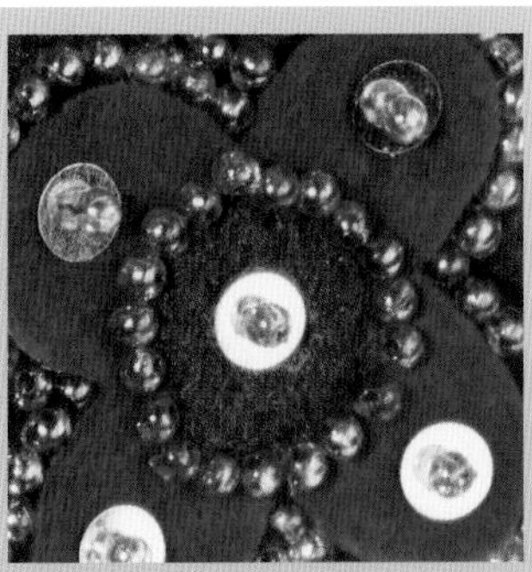

Rainbow Charms★★

Materials required

BRACELET

- *50cm (20in) rat-tail cord*
- *embroidery thread in three matching colours*
- *5 charms*
- *1 button*

Use ringed charms for the bracelet and necklace (see page 83) and charms with holes for the hairclip (see page 82).

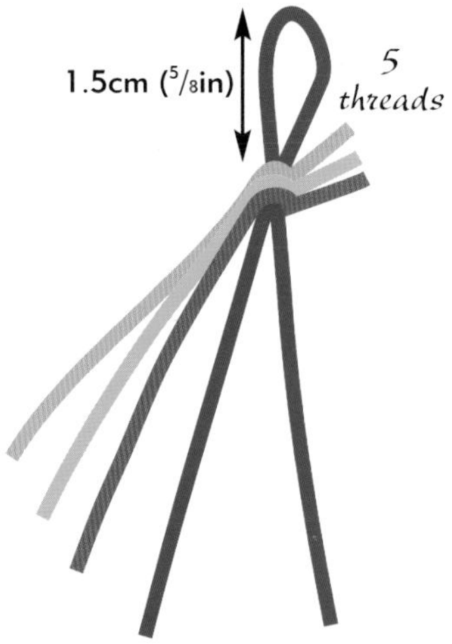
1.5cm ($^{5}/_{8}$in)
5 threads

1 Halve the rat-tail cord and make a 1.5cm ($^{5}/_{8}$in) loop for the button fastening. Cut 1.5m (4ft 11in) lengths of three strands of different coloured embroidery thread. Knot the threads tightly around the loop.

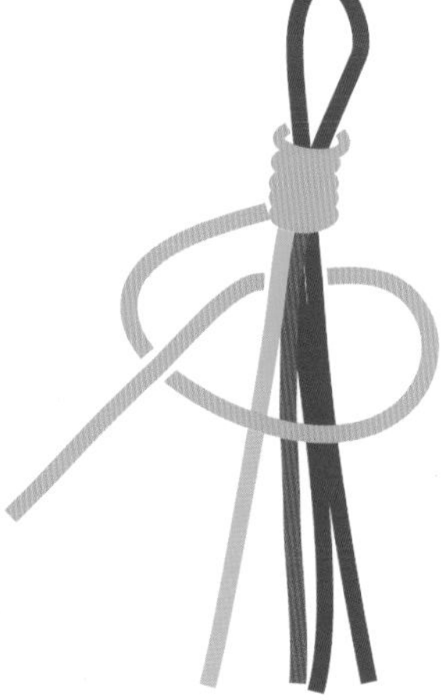

2 Gather the threads to the left of the loop. Select the thread you wish to knot first then bring the other threads together with the rat-tail cord. Wind the selected thread around the cord and other threads, and bring the end through the loop (see diagram above) to make a knot.

These bracelets are quick and easy to make and look stunning if you wear several made from contrasting colours.

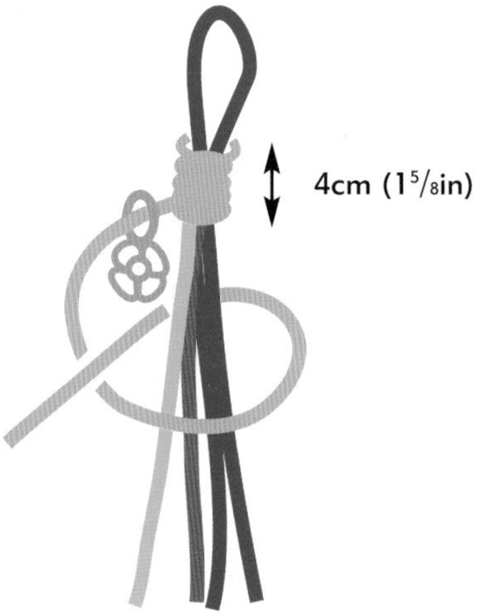
4cm (1$^{5}/_{8}$in)

3 Roughly every 4cm (1$^{5}/_{8}$in), thread on a ringed charm, then continue to make knotted loops.

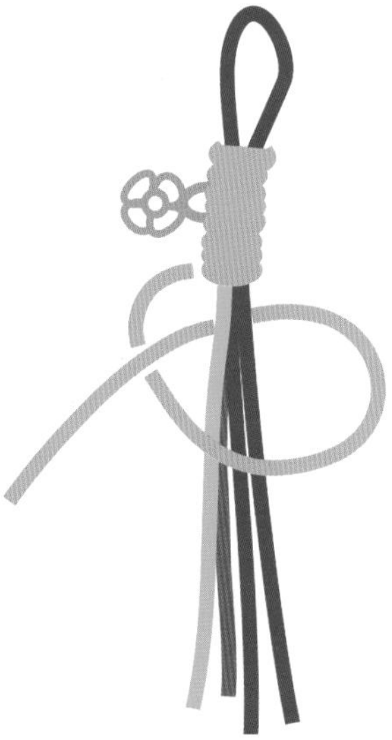

4 To change colours, place the last thread you used back in line with the rat-tail cord and bring out another thread in another colour to the left. Knot it in the same way as you did the first thread. Sew the button to the knotted threads at the opposite end to the loop.

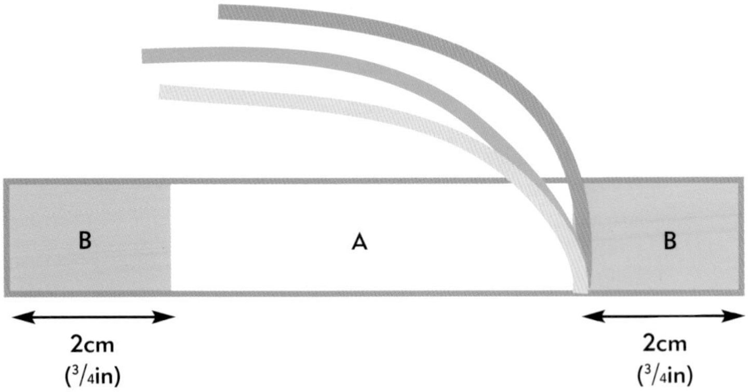
B
A
B
2cm
(3/4in)
2cm
(3/4in)

Materials required

HAIRCLIP

- *foam board*
- *hairclip mount*
- *fabric glue*
- *satin ribbon*
- *3 charms*
- *embroidery thread in three matching colours*

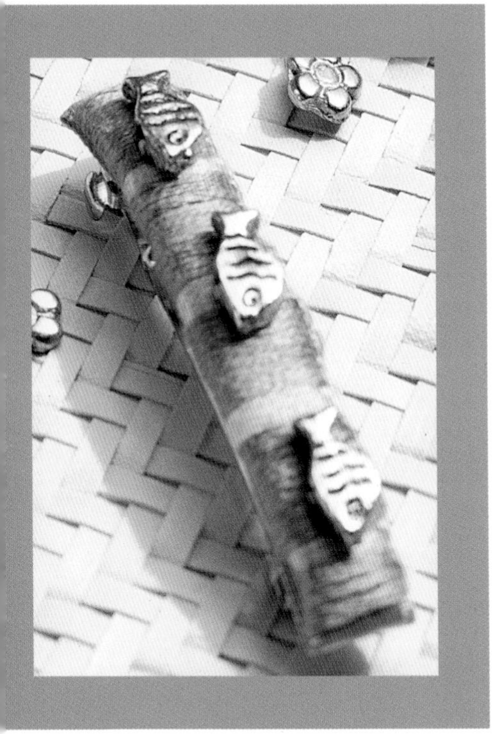

You can decorate this pretty hairclip with many different kinds of motif. To create a matching set of jewellery, opt for charms and threads that match your bracelet or necklace.

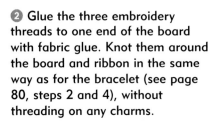

1 Cut the foam board (A) to the same size as the hairclip. Glue to a length of satin ribbon (B) the same width as the hairclip but 4cm ($1\frac{1}{2}$in) longer. Leave 2cm ($\frac{3}{4}$in) satin ribbon at each end.

2 Glue the three embroidery threads to one end of the board with fabric glue. Knot them around the board and ribbon in the same way as for the bracelet (see page 80, steps 2 and 4), without threading on any charms.

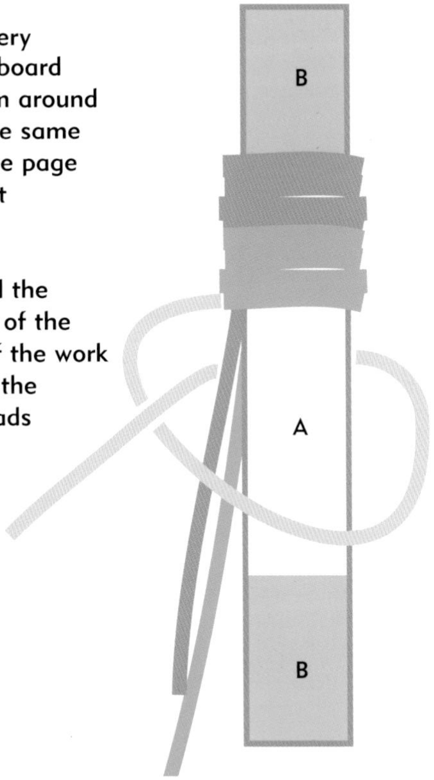
B
A
B

3 When you have covered the foam board, fold the ends of the satin ribbon to the back of the work and glue them down. Sew the charms on top of the threads and glue the strip to the hairclip mount.

B
B

Materials required

NECKLACE

- *1m (39in) rat-tail cord*
- *embroidery thread in three matching colours*
- *8 charms*
- *1 small silver button*

To make up the necklace, follow the instructions for the bracelet (see page 80, steps 1-4).

Ethnic Make-Up Pouch ★★★

Materials required

- *cotton fabric in green, purple, orange, blue and maroon*
- *embroidery thread in orange, purple, green, pale pink, vivid pink and fuchsia*
- *5 washers, 1cm ($^3/_8$in) interior diameter*
- *15cm (6in) of 8mm ($^5/_{16}$in) wide pink satin ribbon*
- *15cm (6in) of 1cm ($^3/_8$in) wide orange satin ribbon*
- *10cm (4in) of 1cm ($^3/_8$in) wide fuchsia velvet ribbon*
- *15cm (6in) of 1cm ($^3/_8$in) wide purple velvet ribbon*
- *thick aluminium sheeting*
- *matching thread, needle*
- *small mother-of-pearl buttons*
- *large blue sequins*
- *small sequins in dark blue, turquoise blue, vivid pink, purple and silver*
- *beads in vivid pink, pale pink, bright blue, pale blue and green*
- *1 button*

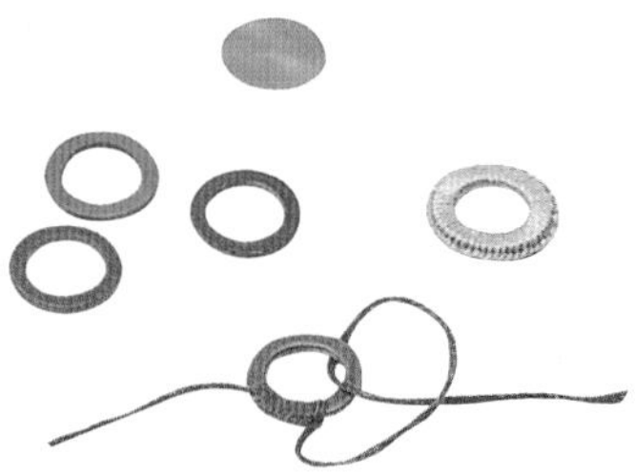

Use leftover scraps of fabric and ribbon to make this pouch. Experiment with colours to create stunning combinations and interplay between tones.

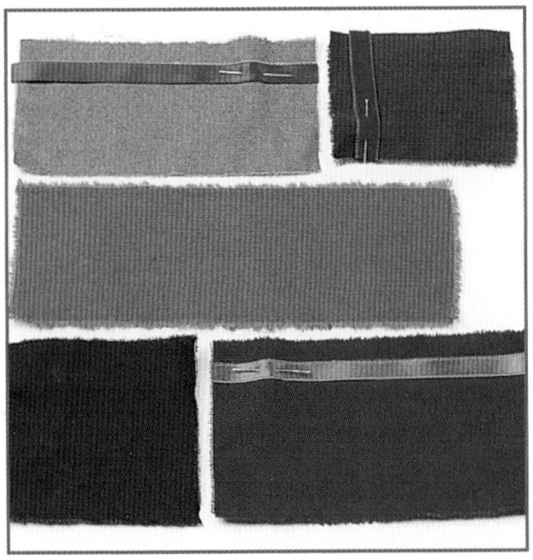

1 Cut the fabric for the patchwork flap. You will need: 12 x 6cm ($4^3/_4$ x $2^3/_8$in) green rectangle, 7 x 6cm ($2^3/_4$ x $2^3/_8$in) purple rectangle, 17 x 6cm ($6^3/_4$ x $2^3/_8$in) orange rectangle, 7cm ($2^3/_4$in) square of blue and 12 x 7cm ($4^3/_4$ x $2^3/_4$in) maroon rectangle. Pin the coloured ribbons on the green, purple and maroon rectangles 1cm ($^3/_8$in) from the edges where the pieces will be assembled, using the photograph above as a guide.

THE FLAP

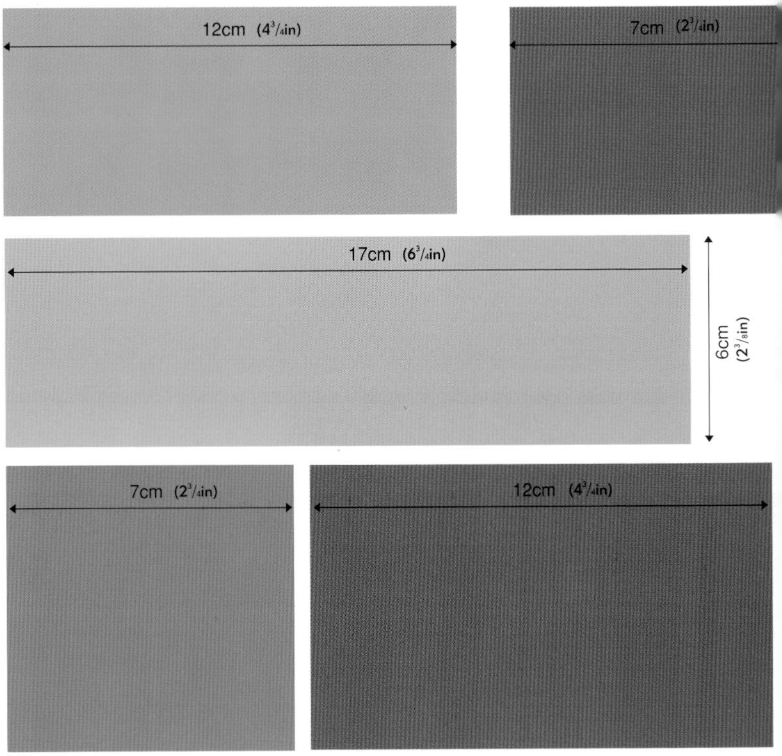
12cm ($4^3/_4$in)
7cm ($2^3/_4$in)
17cm ($6^3/_4$in)
6cm ($2^3/_8$in)
7cm ($2^3/_4$in)
12cm ($4^3/_4$in)

TO MAKE THE FLAP

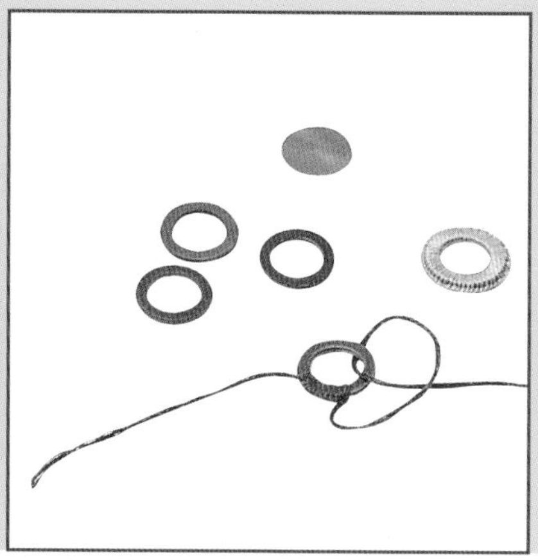
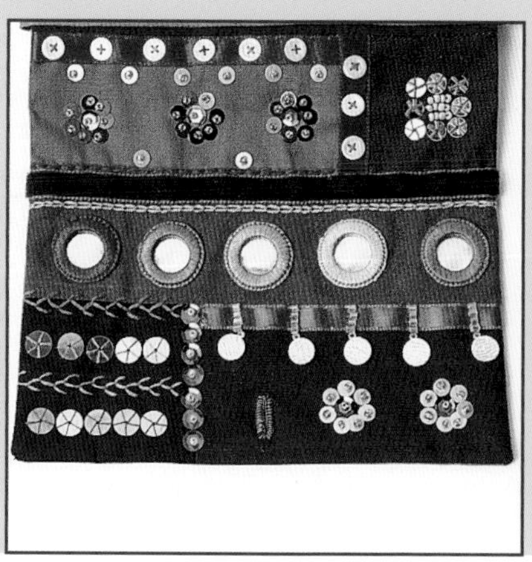

2 Pin the pieces of coloured fabric right sides together, using the photograph above as a guide. Sew together, using 1cm (3/8in) seams. The result is a rectangle 17 x 15cm (6 3/4 x 5 7/8in). Sew the ribbons by hand lengthways along the seams. Sew the purple velvet ribbon to the orange fabric.

3 Make up the rings that will be part of the small mirrors: cut a 1m (39in) length of embroidery thread in each colour and wrap it tightly around the washers with a buttonhole stitch (see page 15). Conceal the start and finish threads by threading them with the needle through the stitches on the reverse of the ring. Cut out five circles from the aluminium sheeting 1.5cm (5/8in) in diameter.

4 Decorate the flap of the pouch with beads, buttons and sequins, using the photograph as a guide. Embroider a row of chain stitch in orange (see page 14) along the upper edge of the purple ribbon and a row of chain stitch in green along the lower edge. Embroider a feather stitch (see page 16) in orange to overlap the orange rectangle and the blue square, and a purple feather stitch between the two rows of large blue sequins. Sew the mirrors on the orange strip, inserting the aluminium circles under the covered washers, and embroider around the outsides with a concealed ladder stitch (see page 17).

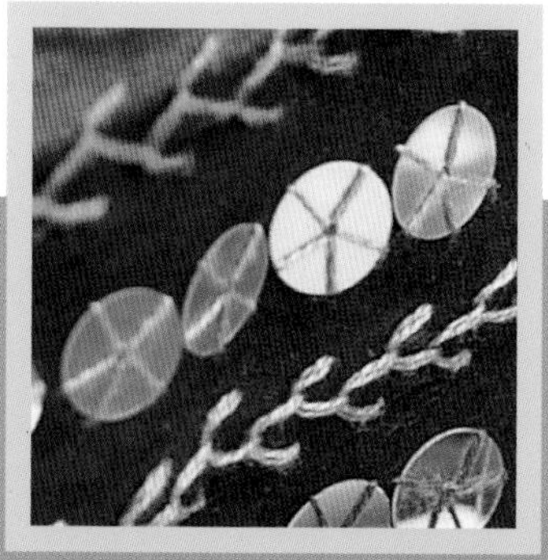

POUCH AND LINING

5 Cut out a 23 x 32cm (9 x 12$^5/_8$in) rectangle of pink fabric for the body of the pouch and a purple rectangle the same size to line it. Fold the pink fabric in half widthways, right sides together, and sew both ends with a 1cm ($^3/_8$in) seam. Make up the bottom of the bag by creating two triangles and sewing along the 6cm (2$^3/_8$in) base of each triangle.

6 Repeat the process with the purple fabric, leaving an 8cm (3$^1/_8$in) opening on one side to allow you to turn the pouch inside out when the seams are finished. Cut out a lining the size of the flap from pink fabric and sew it right sides together around three sides of the flap using a 1cm ($^3/_8$in) seam. Turn the bag inside out and sew it to the lining and flap with a single seam all around the upper edge of the bag.

7 Turn the pouch inside out through the 8cm (3$^1/_8$in) opening in the lining and sew up with ladder stitch (see page 17). Make a buttonhole in the flap by making a slit through the two pieces of fabric and neatening with buttonhole stitch (see page 15). Sew a button onto the bag.

Why not make a more lavish pouch in silk patchwork? You can make it larger by altering the dimensions to suit your requirements.

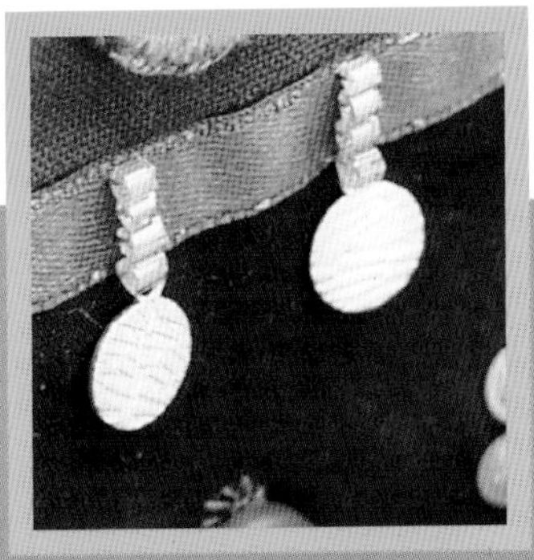

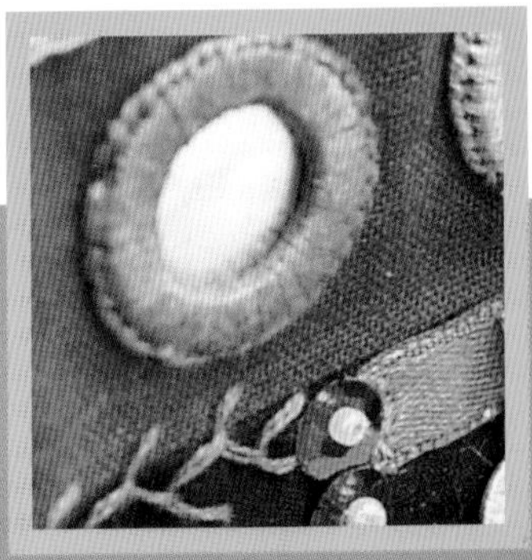

Embroidered Butterfly Bags ★★★

Materials required

PINK BEAD BAG

- *8.5 x 17cm (3³/8in x 6³/4in) pink silk*
- *small glass beads in red, pale blue, darker blue, pink and bronze*
- *a long needle*
- *canvas*
- *white and pink thread*
- *embroidery hoop*

Ensure that you cut out a piece of canvas that is large enough to stretch over the embroidery hoop.

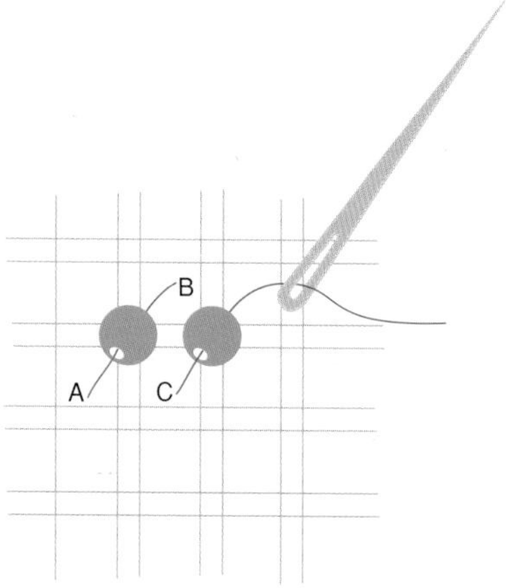

B
A
C

1 Cut out a square of canvas and fix it in the embroidery hoop. Embroider a 6.5cm (2½in) square (see pattern on page 90), with the butterfly motif centred in the square. Bring the needle through from the wrong side of the canvas at A (see diagram above), thread on the bead, insert the needle in at B and come up again at C.

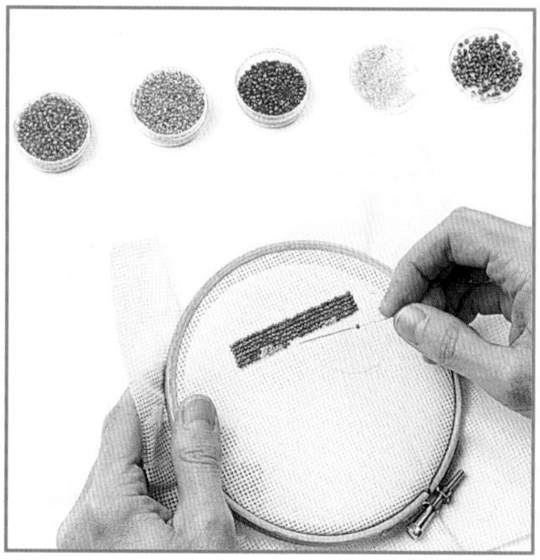

2 Start with the red background beads, sewing left to right and top to bottom. Include the butterfly using the colours suggested in the pattern on page 90 or choosing an alternative combination.

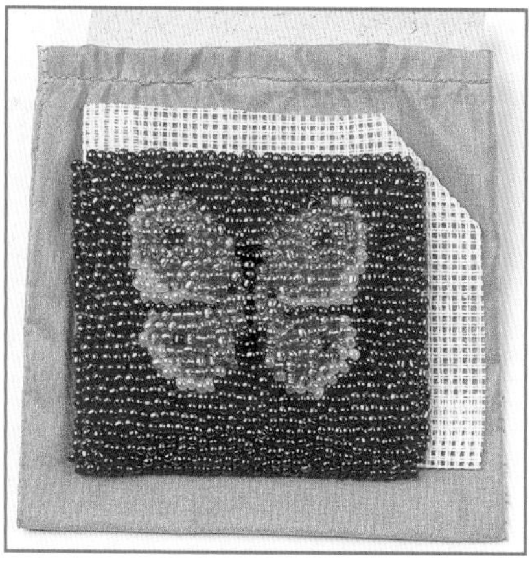

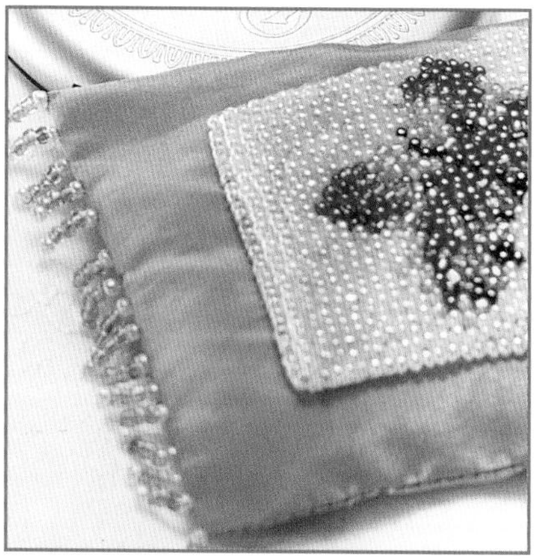

3 Fold the pink fabric in half to make an 8.5cm (3³/8in) square. Stitch French seams along two edges (see page 17). Cut around the beaded motif leaving a margin of 1.5cm (5/8in). Fold the edges to the back, and sew the pocket to the front of the bag using ladder stitch (see page 17). Slip a piece of cardboard inside the bag to prevent sewing the two layers of material together. Neaten the top of the bag with a seam and then embroider a row of beads 0.6cm (¼in) from the upper edge to disguise the seam, alternating three of the red beads with one blue bead.

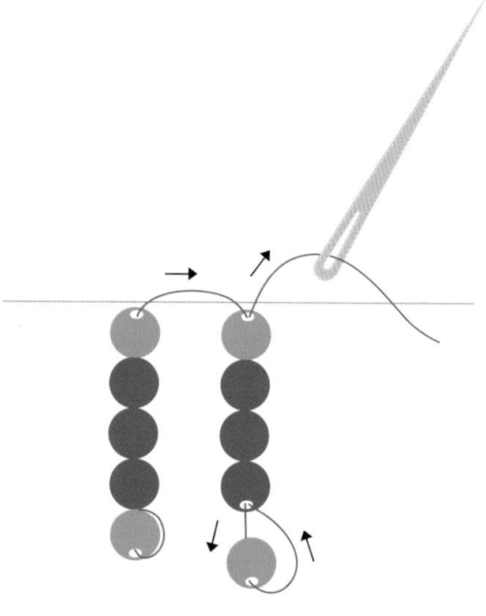

4 Make a fringe of beads at the bottom of the bag following the diagram above. Next, thread pink beads on to a 60cm (24in) length of thread to make the shoulder strap. Fix the strap to the inside of the bag with a small stitch, positioned on the side seam.

PARIS

The pattern for the pink bead bag is made up of 35 rows of 35 small glass beads. Work from top to bottom and from left to right.

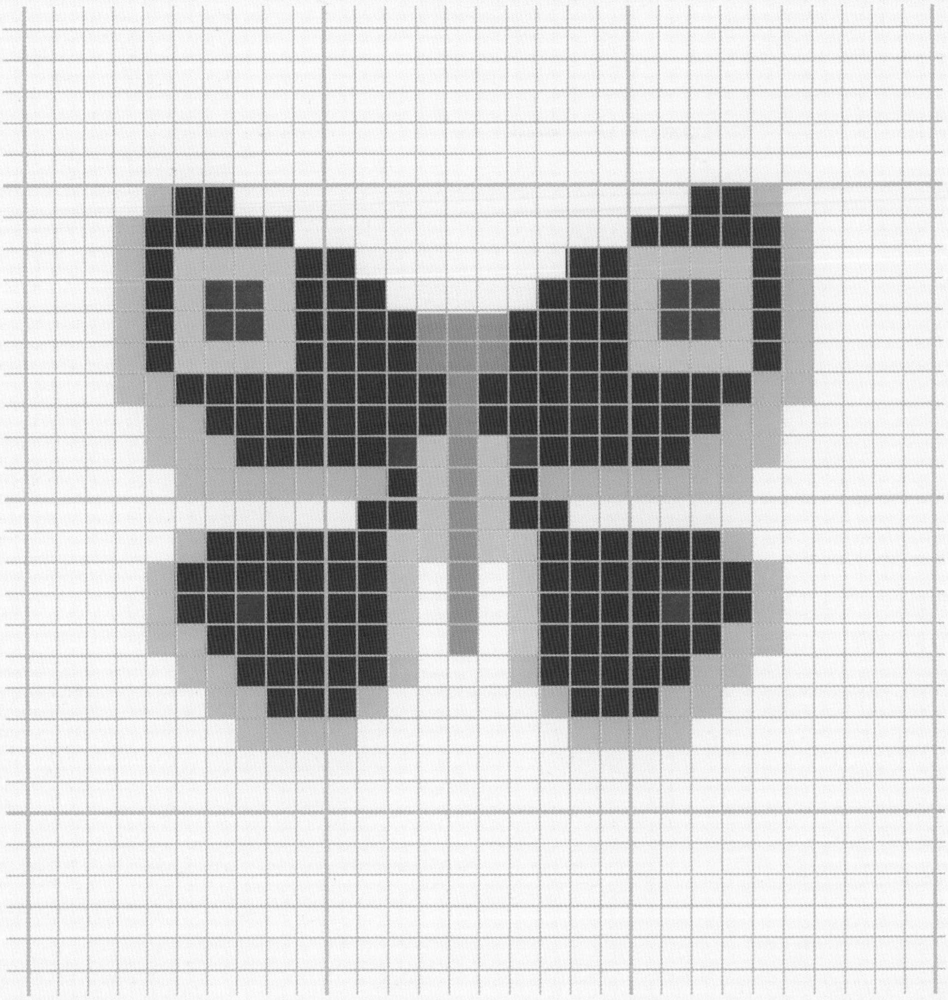

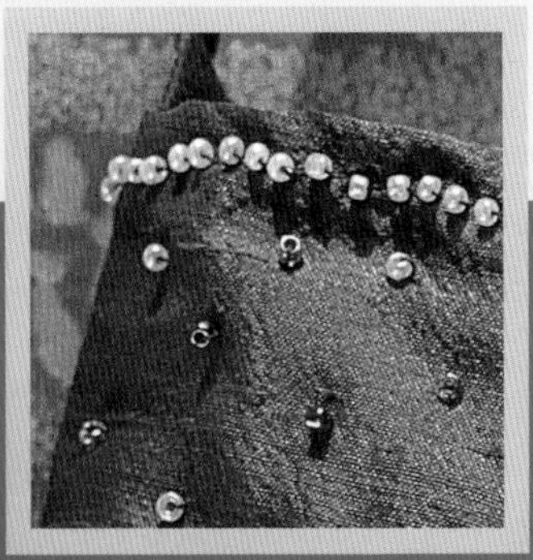

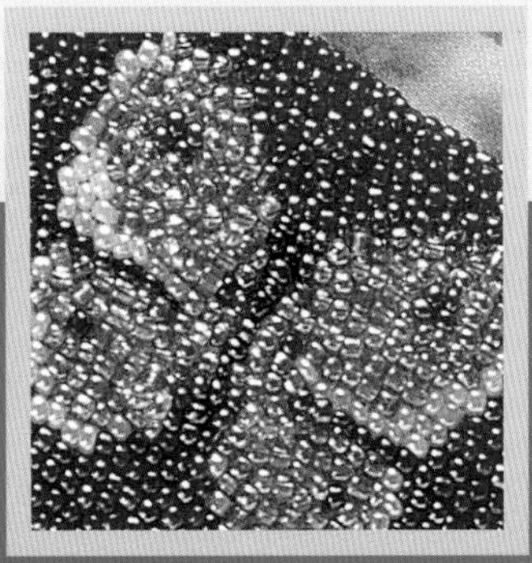

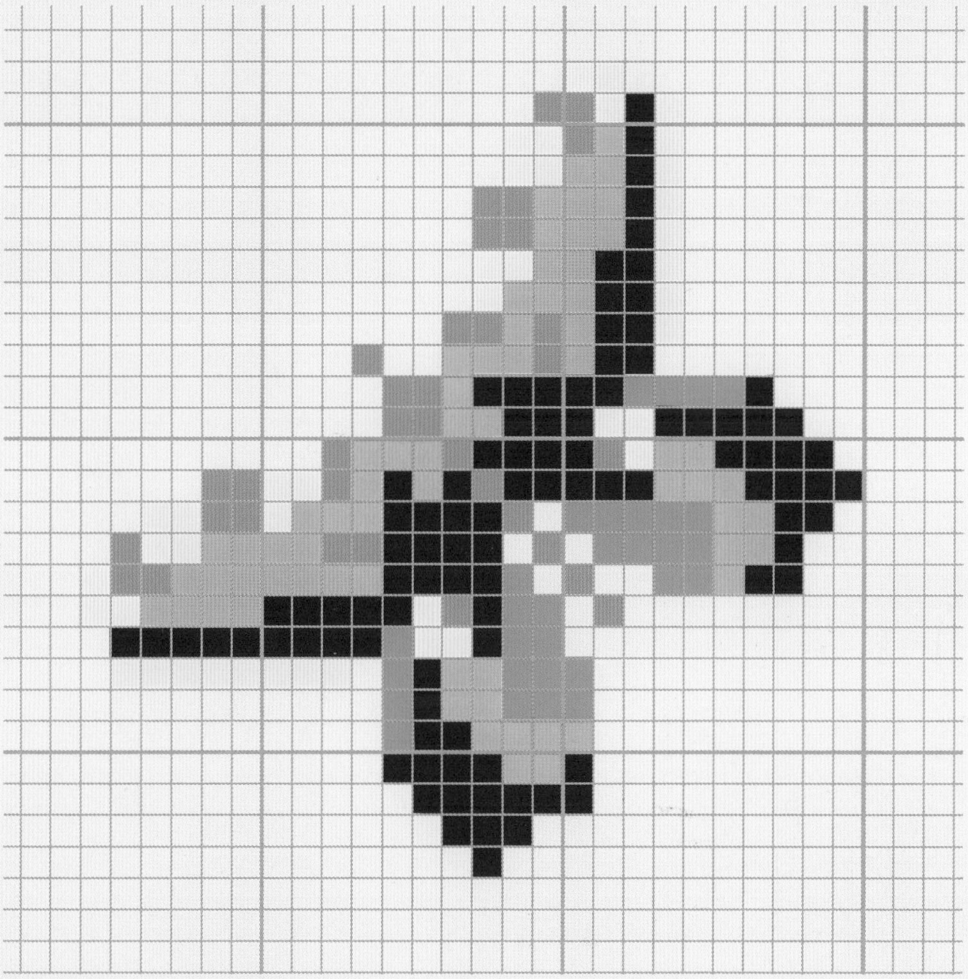

Butterfly pattern for the small blue bead bag.

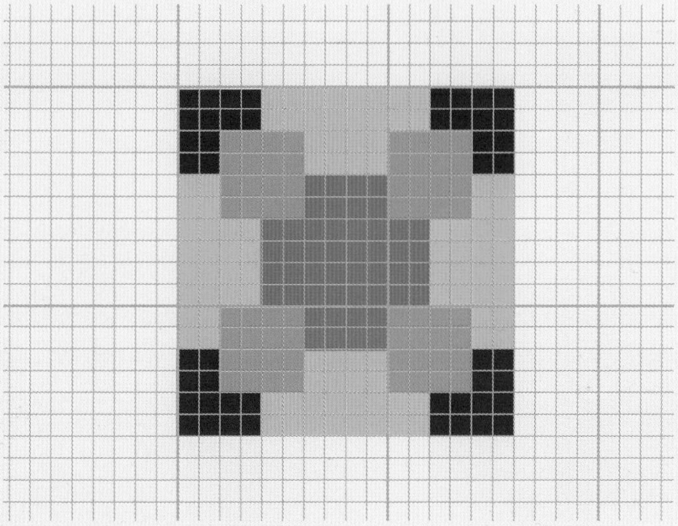

Small geometric pattern for the purple bead bag.

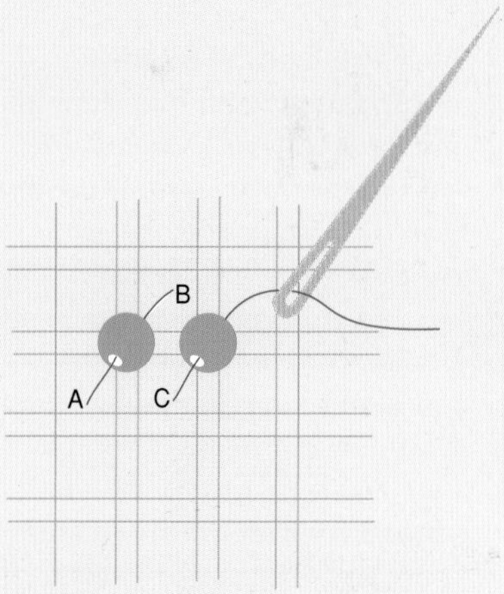
B
A
C

Sewing on the beads (see page 88, step 1).

Andalusian Headscarf ★

Materials required

SCARF

- *60cm (24in) square pink cotton*
- *embroidery thread in blue and green*
- *small glass beads in pink, blue and green*
- *flat sequins 1cm ($^3/_8$in) in diameter*
- *a needle*

Adapt the size of the triangle to the size of your head: these scarves are prettier if they are fairly small.

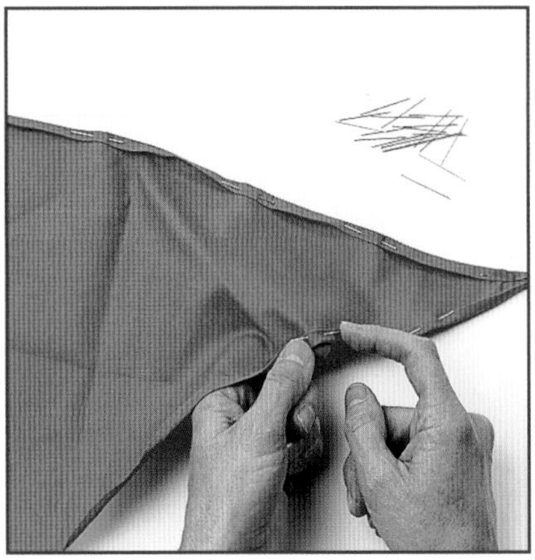

1 Cut out an isosceles triangle with 53cm (21in) sides (see page 109) from the pink cotton. Cut the point at around 1cm ($^3/_8$in) at each acute angle, to reduce the bulk of the material. Fold 0.5cm ($^3/_{16}$in) under twice, all around the edge. Press with a hot iron and pin.

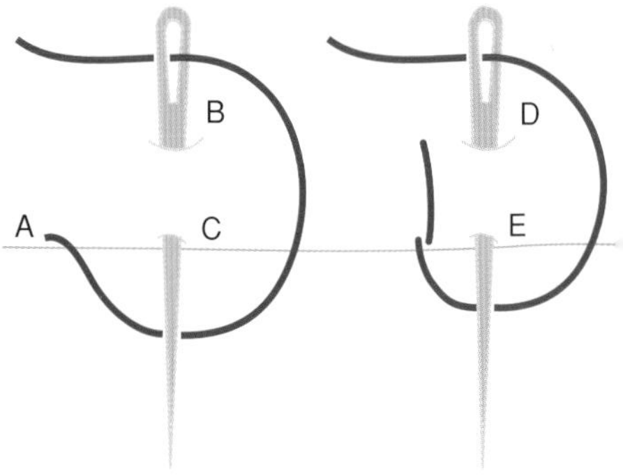
A
B
C
D
E

2 On the right side, sew blanket stitch (see page 15) around the outside edge with blue thread. Sew the stitches at 0.6cm ($^1/_4$in) intervals. This blanket stitch will hold the hem in place. Remove the pins as you go.

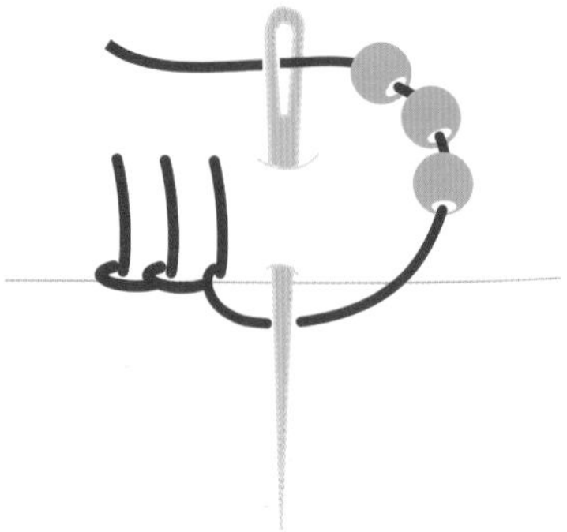

3 Every three or four stitches, thread three blue, pink or green beads on to the thread as shown in the diagram above.

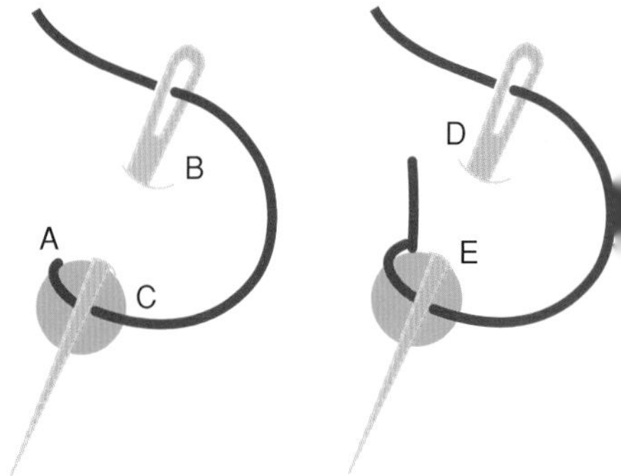
A
B
C
D
E

4 Sew on sequins, securing each one with a small glass bead (see page 74, diagram E). Embroider around each sequin with blanket stitch following the diagram above, and using alternate blue and green thread.

You could use other light materials to make these small headscarves, such as cotton voile or fine wool. Avoid using materials that are shiny and therefore slippery.

The black fleece headscarf is quick and easy to make. There is no need to hem, as fleece does not fray. Embroider the edges with blanket stitch (see page 15) with added beads.

The bag measures 15cm (6in) square. The edges are seamed using blanket stitch (see page 15). The shoulder strap is 90 x 2.5cm ($35^1/_2$ x 1in).

Ribboned Stole ★★

Materials required

- *107 x 44cm (3ft 6in x $17^{3}/_{8}$in) rectangle of green silk taffeta*
- *50cm (20in) of 2cm ($^{3}/_{4}$in) wide yellow sheer ribbon*
- *50cm (20in) of 2cm ($^{3}/_{4}$in) wide dark green sheer ribbon*
- *50cm (20in) of 2cm ($^{3}/_{4}$in) wide pale green sheer ribbon*
- *1m (39in) of 8mm ($^{5}/_{16}$in) wide yellow satin ribbon*
- *1m (39in) of 1.5cm ($^{5}/_{8}$in) wide green satin ribbon*
- *small glass beads in green*
- *flat sequins*
- *needle*
- *thread*

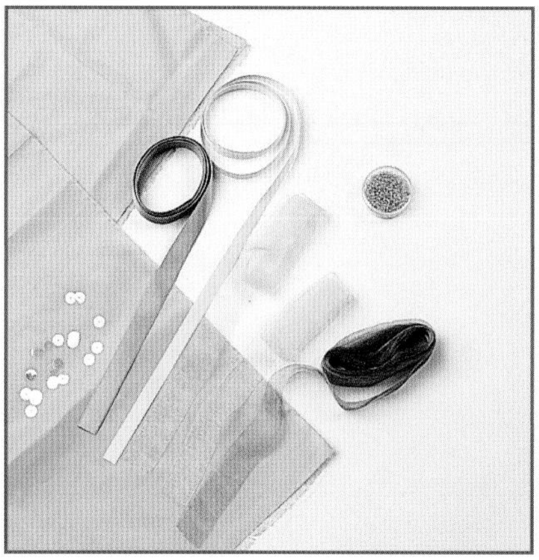

1 Cut the taffeta to obtain two strips 107 x 22cm (3ft 6in x $8^{5}/_{8}$in). Attach the ribbons to one of the strips, and use the other for the lining.

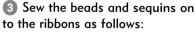

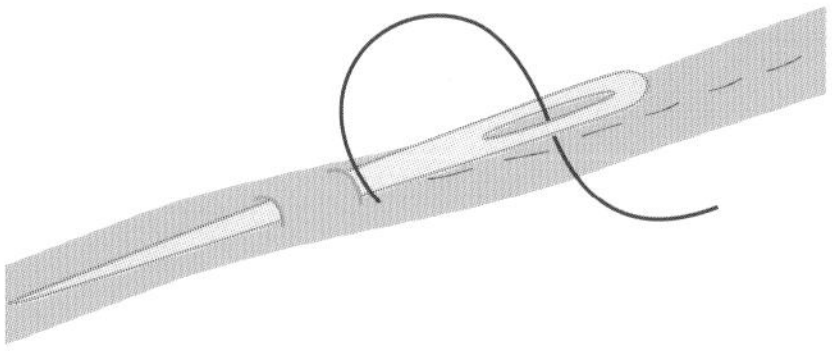

2 Starting 2cm ($^{3}/_{4}$in) from one short edge of the stole, pin the ribbons on in the following order:
– 1 yellow sheer ribbon,
– 1 green satin ribbon,
– 1 dark green sheer ribbon,
– 1 yellow satin ribbon,
– 1 pale green sheer ribbon
– 1 green satin ribbon.
Secure the sheer ribbons by sewing the satin ribbons to the scarf using very small backstitch (see diagram above). Do the same at the other end of the scarf.

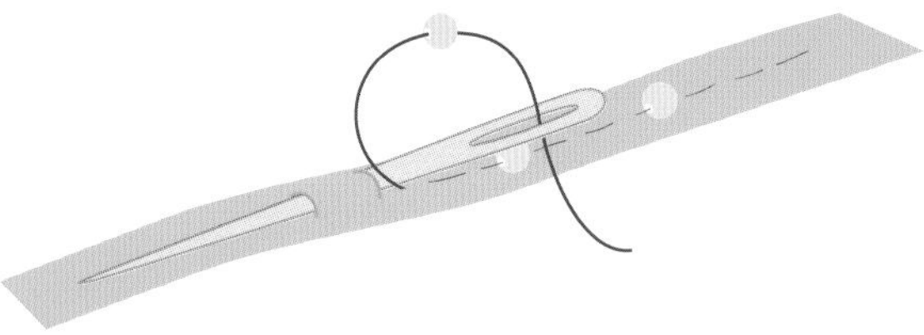

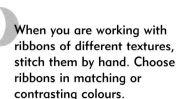

When you are working with ribbons of different textures, stitch them by hand. Choose ribbons in matching or contrasting colours.

Why not make scarves in velvet or wool for cold winter days?
The bag measures 21 x 18cm ($8^{1}/_{4}$ x $7^{1}/_{8}$in) and the ribbons are sewn on in the same way before the bag is assembled.
The shoulder strap is made from two lengths of red cord 105cm ($41^{1}/_{2}$in) long.

3 Sew the beads and sequins on to the ribbons as follows:
– Scatter the green beads over the yellow sheer ribbon.
– Sew a row of beads at 1cm ($^{3}/_{8}$in) intervals along the lower edge of the green satin ribbon.
– Sew the flat sequins to the dark green sheer ribbon, securing each one with a bead (see Designer Motif T-Shirts, page 96, step 4) at roughly 1cm ($^{3}/_{8}$in) intervals.
– Sew a row of beads at roughly 1cm ($^{3}/_{8}$in) intervals on the lower edge of the yellow satin ribbon.
– Sew a few beads on the pale green sheer ribbon at random.
– Sew a row of beads at 1cm ($^{3}/_{8}$in) intervals on the lower edge of the green satin ribbon.

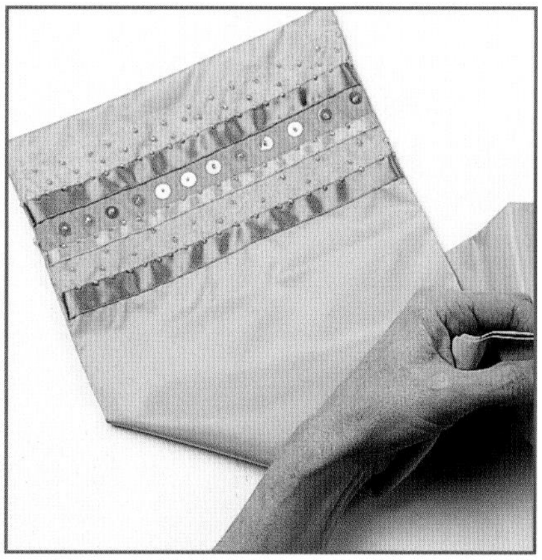

4 Place the two sides of the stole right sides together and stitch with a sewing machine, leaving an opening of about 15cm (6in). Turn the stole right side out. Press the seams with an iron and close the opening neatly with ladder stitch (see page 17).

Designer Motif T-Shirts★★

Materials required

- *T-shirt*
- *dressmaker's pencil*
- *glitter fabric pen in gold or silver*
- *fine needle*
- *thread to match T-shirt*
- *bugles*
- *small perforated sequins*
- *clear or coloured small glass beads*

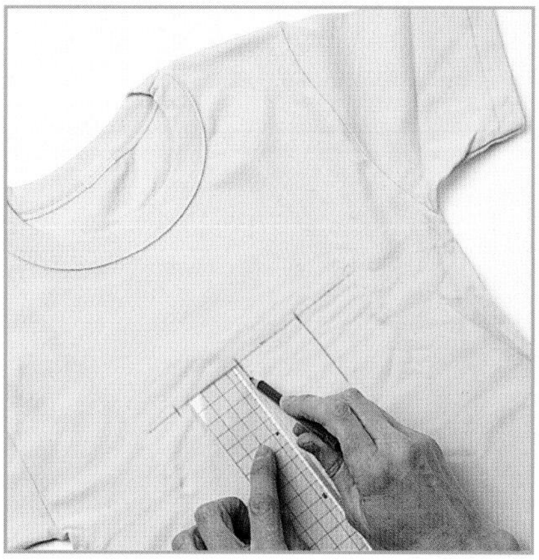

1 Mark a 12cm (4$^3/_4$in) line using the dressmaker's pencil below the neckline of the T-shirt. Mark the centre of the line and 5cm (2in) each side of the centre. Trace off the design of your choice (see page 110) and transfer to the T-shirt.

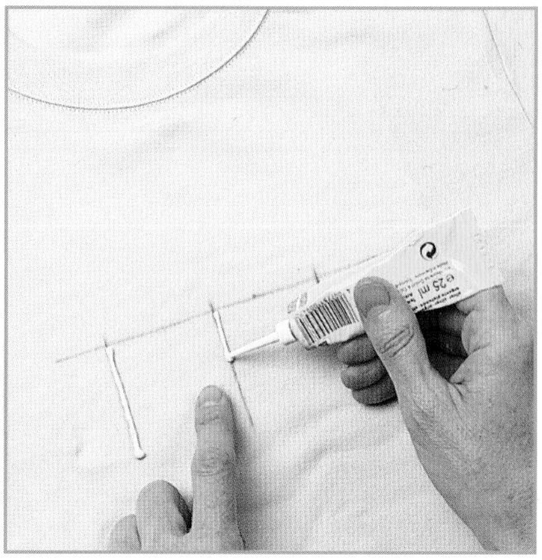

25 ml

2 Place a piece of card inside the T-shirt to avoid staining the back. Go over your chosen design with the glitter pen. Squeeze the tube gently as you go and leave to dry for at least half an hour.

To make other T-shirts, take your inspiration from the designs on page 110, and to complete your outfit, why not repeat the design on a bag, scarf or purse?

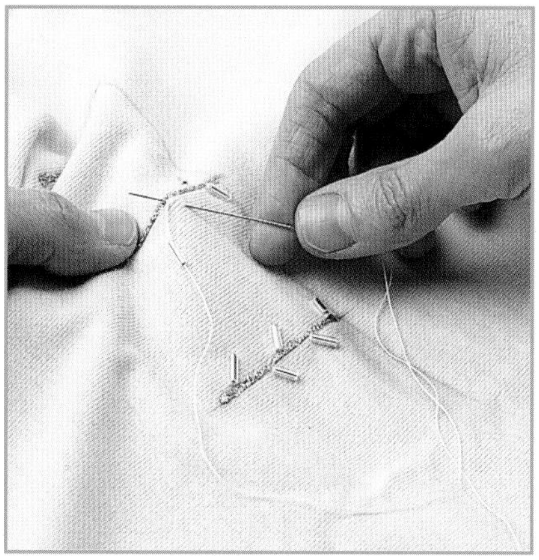

3 Bring a needle and thread through from the wrong side of the fabric and thread on a bugle. Take the needle through the bead twice to secure it. Continue in this way and finish with a double stitch on the wrong side of the fabric.

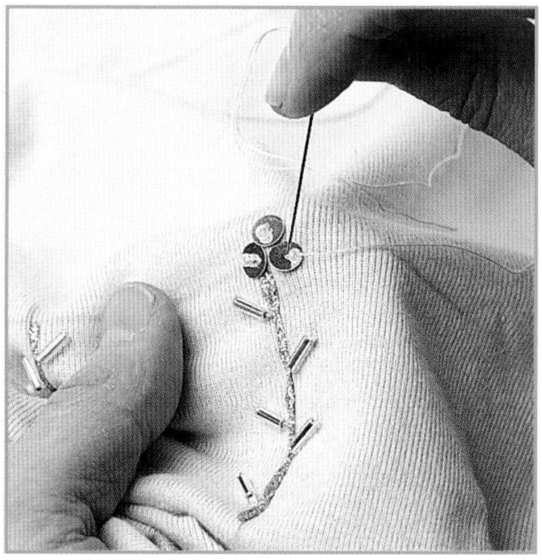

4 Bring the needle and thread through from the wrong side of the fabric and thread on a sequin and then a bead. Go back over the bead and through the sequin, and secure with a double stitch on the wrong side of the fabric.

Starry Night Candleholders

Materials required

- *16 x 29cm (6¼ x 11½in) rectangle of tarlatan*
- *bone folder*
- *fine needle*
- *fabric glue*
- *thread to match the tarlatan*
- *perforated sequins*
- *small glass beads*
- *glass yoghurt pot*
- *tealight*

Always place the candle in a glass container inside the candleholder.

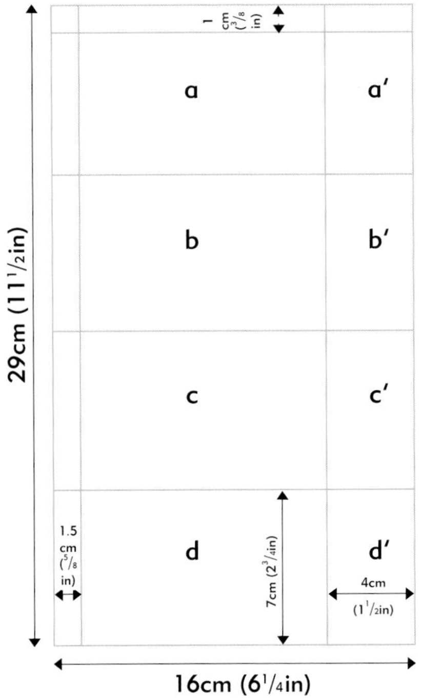
1 cm (3/8 in)
a
a'
b
b'
c
c'
d
d'
1.5 cm (5/8 in)
7cm (2 3/4in)
4cm (1 1/2in)
29cm (11 1/2in)
16cm (6 1/4in)

1 Mark the folds on the tarlatan following the dimensions shown on the diagram above, making creases with the bone folder.

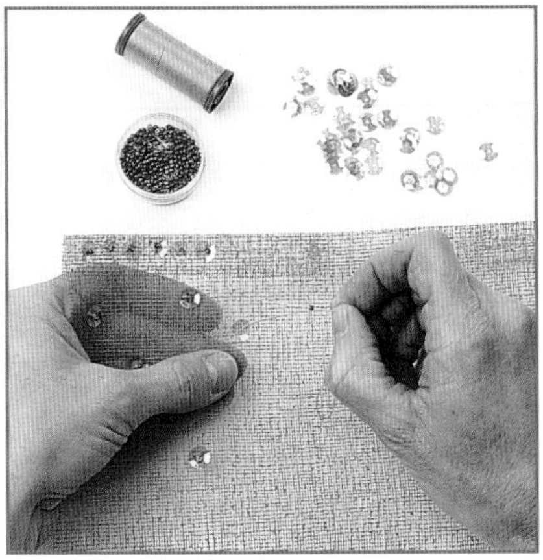

2 Decorate the four sides of the candleholder (a, b, c and d) with sequins and beads: tie a small knot in the thread, bring the needle and thread through from the wrong side, thread on a sequin and bead and go back through the hole of the sequin. Secure with a double stitch behind the sequin on the wrong side of the tarlatan.

If you only have white tarlatan you can dye it with a dampened roller and some coloured inks diluted in water.

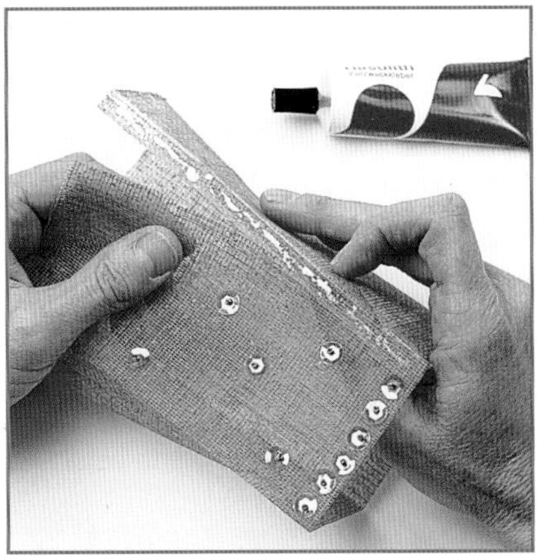

3 Fold the top edge under by 1.5cm (5/8in) (see diagram above) and the raw edge under by 0.6cm (1/4in). Secure with sequins. Glue the flap to the other edge. Leave to dry for 5 minutes.

4 To form the bottom of the candle holder, fold down the 4cm (1½in) high side (a') towards the centre and fold down the opposite side (c') on top of it. You will have two triangles on each side (b' and d') which you can then fold down on to the bottom of the candleholder, pressing gently.

Garland of Gold and Light*

Materials required

TWO SHADES

- *circle of card 17cm (6$\frac{3}{4}$in) in diameter*
- *white dressmaker's pencil*
- *1m (39in) gold organza with orange shimmer*
- *scissors*
- *small glass beads in orange, gold and iridescent*
- *fine needle*
- *fine gold thread*
- *string of white fairy lights*
- *thick gold thread*

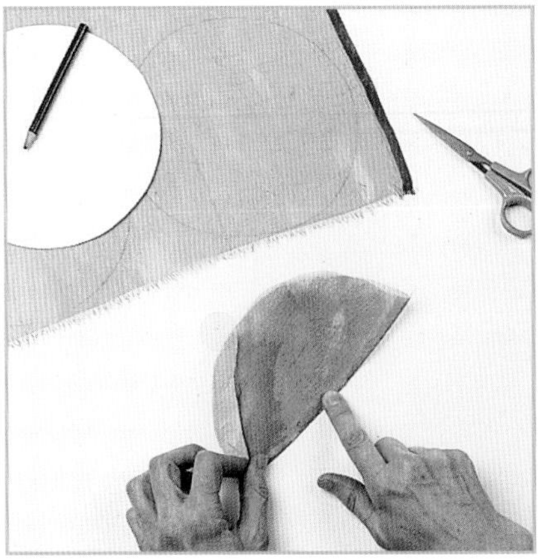

1 Mark a circle on the organza using the dressmaker's pencil, and cut out. Fold the circle in half, creasing to mark and cut in half.

2 Sew beads around the edge of the arc of each semicircle, using fine gold thread. Alternate the three colours as you work.

Lightly iron the semicircles before sewing on the beads.

You could also make these decorations in white or coloured tarlatan.

3 Make a cone, overlapping the edges by 0.5cm ($\frac{1}{4}$in) and securing with a row of beads, starting from the base of the cone. Stop 2cm ($\frac{3}{4}$in) from the tip of the cone.

4 Place the opening in the cone over a bulb. Thread the needle with thick gold thread and pass it through the edges of the material twice. Remove the needle, loop the gold thread around the electric wire and tie a pretty knot to attach it firmly.

Sparkling Lampshade

Materials required

- *1 metal lampshade frame, 10cm (4in) in diameter*
- *1 reel of stainless steel wire, 0.3mm (1/64in) in diameter*
- *wire cutters*
- *3 types of small glass beads*
- *3 types of large beads*
- *2 types of perforated sequins*
- *2 types of medium-sized beads*
- *2 types of bugles*

You can use any kind of lampshade regardless of size for this project, providing the shade has vertical legs.

1 Assemble the lampshade frame, wire cutters and thin stainless steel, as well as the assorted beads. Clear or iridescent beads are especially suited to this project as they catch the light well. Choose a variety of colours and shapes.

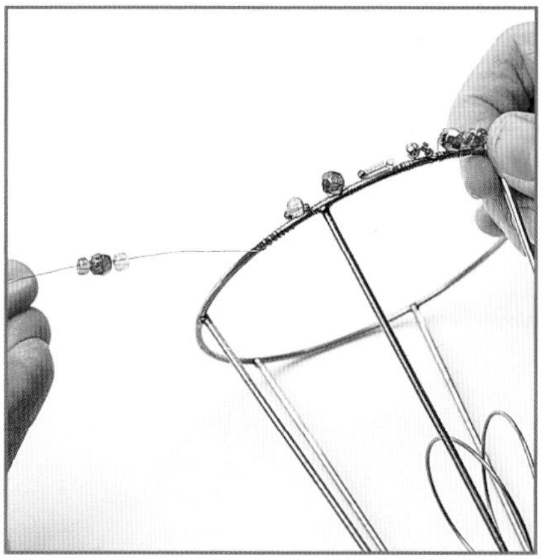

2 Cut a 1m (39in) length of stainless steel wire and wind one end tightly around the wide circular end of the frame four times. Thread on between one and five beads and wind the thread six times tightly around the frame. Continue around the circle, then repeat this process around the smaller circle at the other end of the shade.

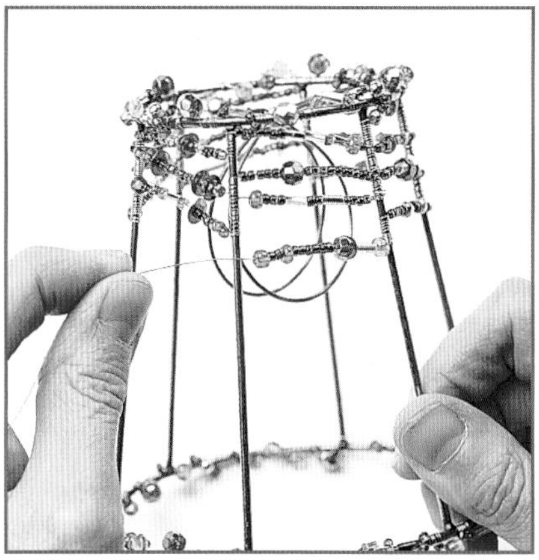

3 To decorate the lampshade, cut a 1m (39in) length of stainless steel wire and wind it four times tightly around one of the vertical legs of the frame. Thread on a string of beads, alternating colours and shapes.
On the next vertical leg wind the stainless steel wire around ten times very tightly. Continue around the lampshade until you reach the base.

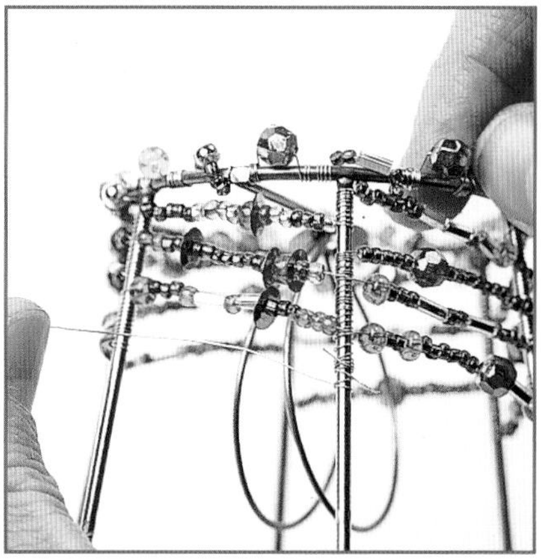

4 When a length of wire is finished, pull the end tightly and wind five times around the vertical leg. Start again from the same point, winding the new wire around five times.

Flowered Felt Cushions ★★

Materials required

CUSHION

- *34 x 34 cm (14¼ x 13½in) red felt, 34 x 20cm (13½ x 8in) purple felt, 38 x 34cm (15 x 13½in) brown felt*
- *needle and purple thread*
- *blue and iridescent small glass beads*
- *dressmaker's pencil*
- *piece of thin card*

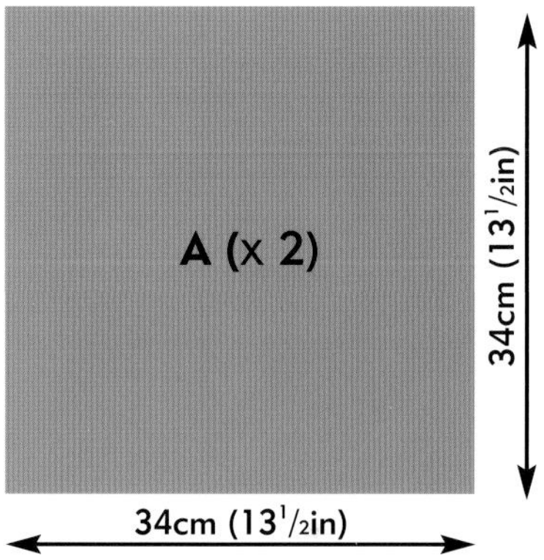
A (x 2)
34cm (13½in)
34cm (13½in)

1. Cut out two 34cm (13½in) felt squares in red and brown (see diagram A). Cut out four strips of purple felt, 4 x 34cm (1½ x 13½in); cut the ends at 45° angles (see diagram B). Cut out four red strips (to use as ties) 0.6 x 18cm (¼ x 7⅞in) (see diagram C).

B (x 4)

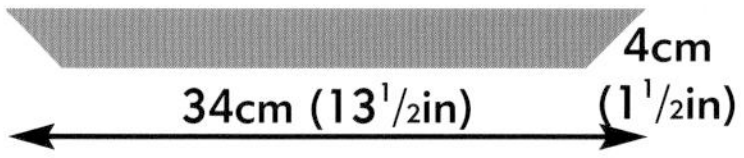
4cm
(1½in)
34cm (13½in)

C (x 4)

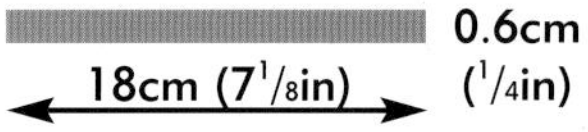
0.6cm
(¼in)
18cm (7⅞in)

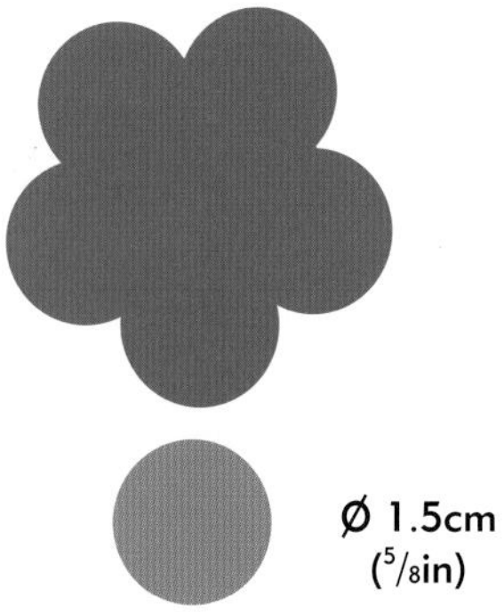
Ø 1.5cm
(⅝in)

D (x 4)

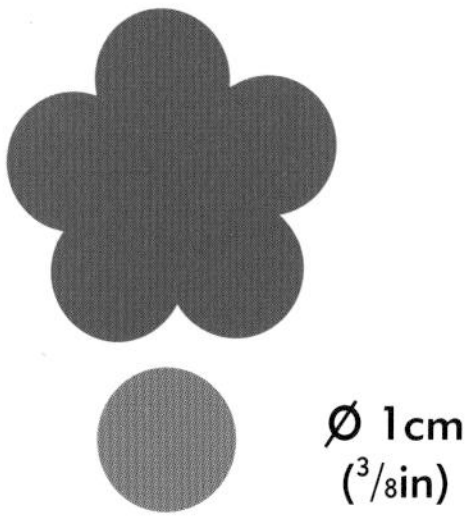
Ø 1cm
(⅜in)

E (x 8)

2. Trace off and cut out four large purple flowers (see diagram D) and eight small flowers (see diagram E), using the templates as a guide. Cut out eight circles 1cm (⅜in) in diameter (see diagram E) and four circles 1.5cm (⅝in) in diameter (see diagram D) from the brown felt, to form the centre of the flowers.

Trace off the flower templates above, transfer to the card then place on the felt and draw around them, before cutting out.

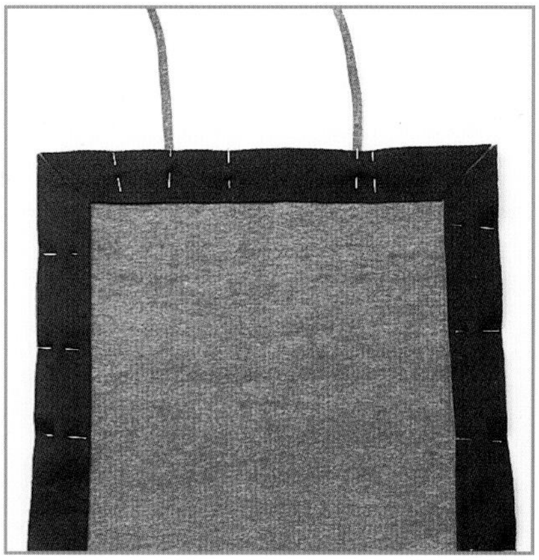

3. Pin two ties on the wrong side of the red square 11cm (4⅜in) from the corners. Working on the wrong side of the fabric, pin the purple strips along the four edges and sew in place 2cm (¾in) from the edge using the purple thread.

These cushion covers are very decorative. Display one or two flowered cushions with other plain cushions of the same colour.

Wrong side of brown square

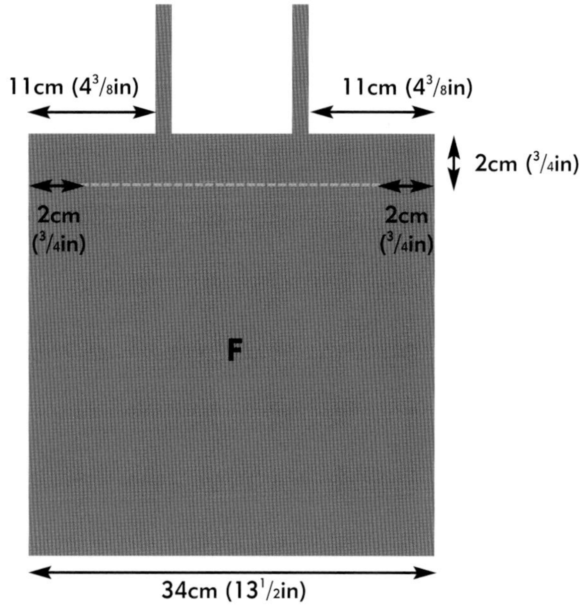
11cm (4 3/8in)
11cm (4 3/8in)
2cm (3/4in)
2cm (3/4in)
2cm (3/4in)
F
34cm (13 1/2in)

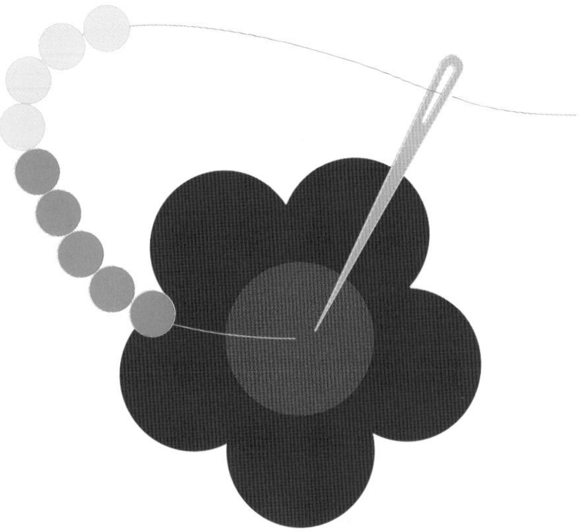

G

4 Pin the other two ties on the wrong side of the brown square (see diagram F). Mark 2cm (3/4in) below the top edge and sew a row of running stitch – with a machine or by hand.

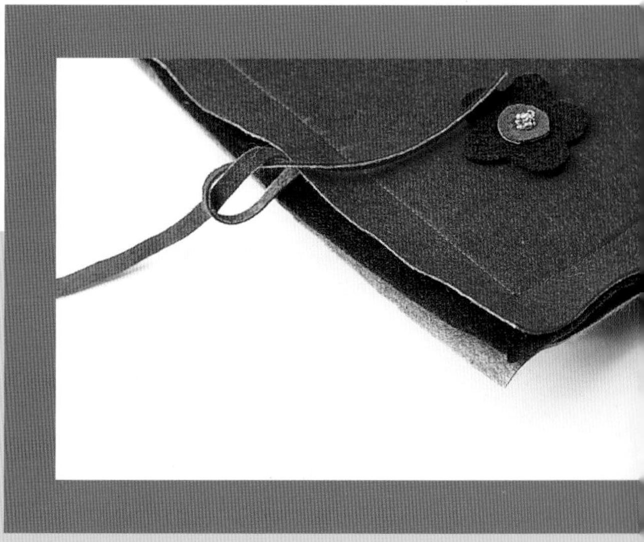

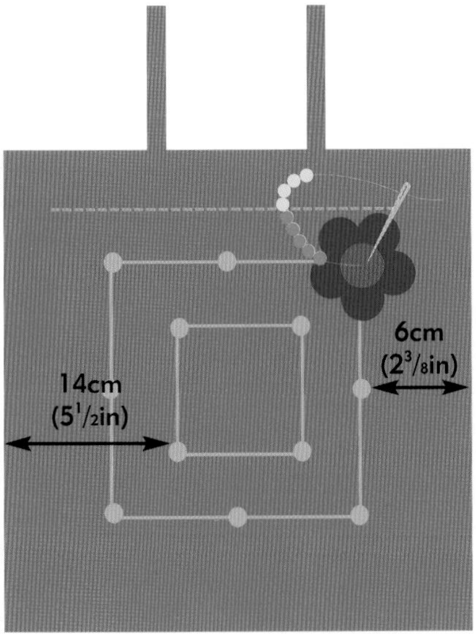
14cm
(5½in)
6cm
(2⅜in)

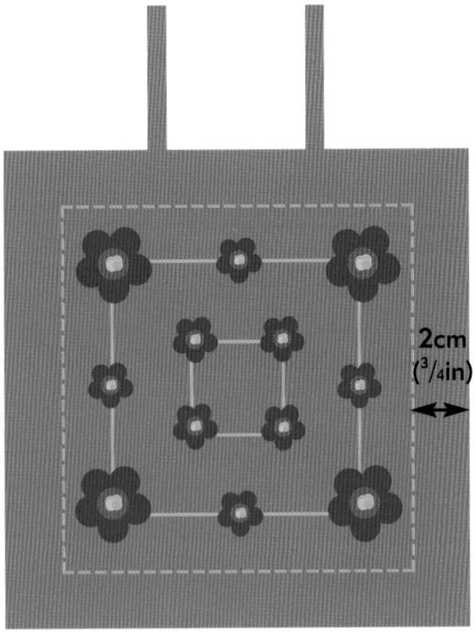
2cm
(¾in)

5 Arrange the large and small flowers and centres on the right side of the red felt square (see diagrams above). Secure the large flowers with a cluster of five blue and four iridescent beads (see page 106, diagram G).

6 Secure the small flowers with a cluster of three blue and two iridescent beads. Place the red and brown felt squares wrong sides together and seam 2cm (¾in) from three edges with purple thread, leaving the top open.

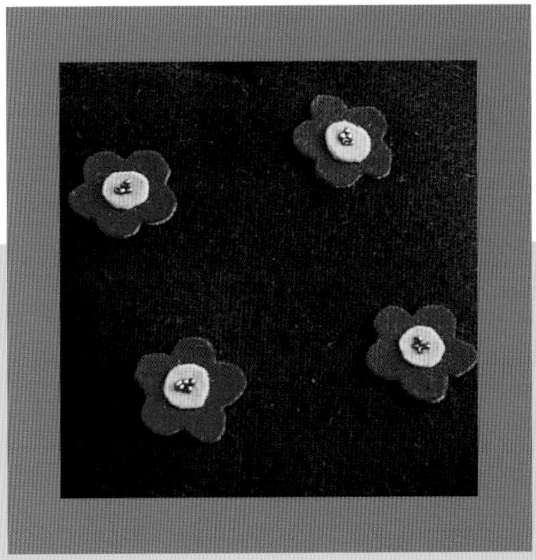

BEADED FLOWER MOTIFS (SEE PAGE 64)

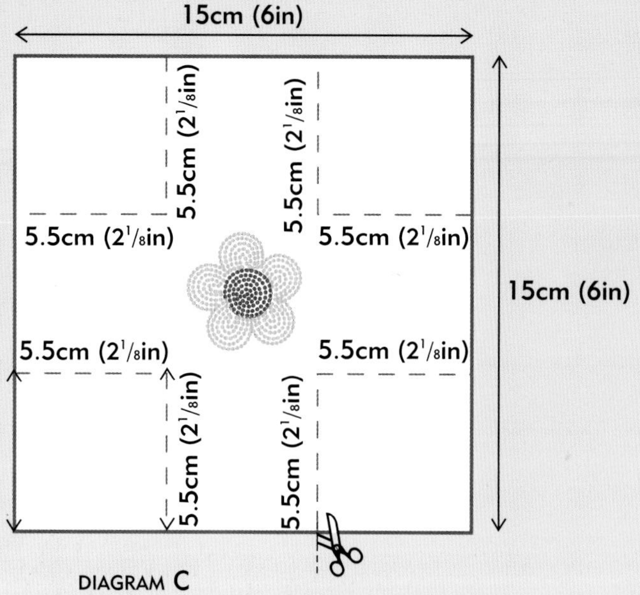
15cm (6in)
15cm (6in)
5.5cm (2 1/8in)
5.5cm (2 1/8in)
5.5cm (2 1/8in)
5.5cm (2 1/8in)
5.5cm (2 1/8in)
5.5cm (2 1/8in)
5.5cm (2 1/8in)
5.5cm (2 1/8in)

DIAGRAM C

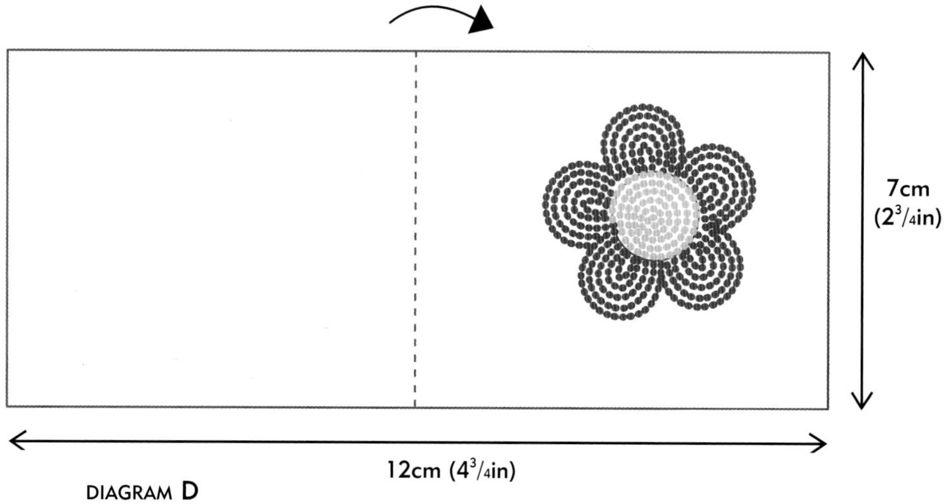
7cm
(2 3/4in)
12cm (4 3/4in)

DIAGRAM D

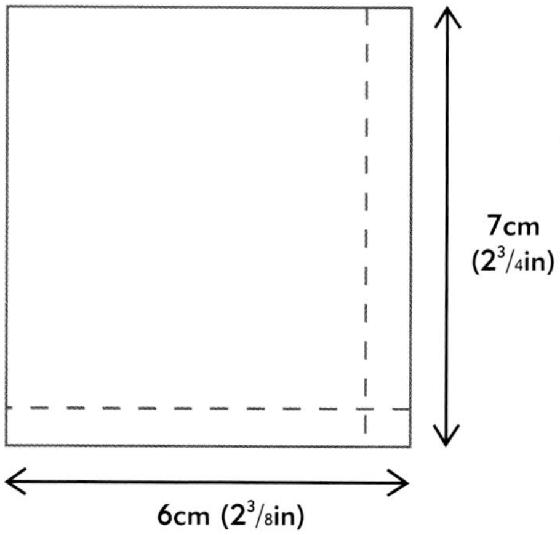
7cm
(2 3/4in)
6cm (2 3/8in)

DIAGRAM E

Silk Flowers (see page 66)

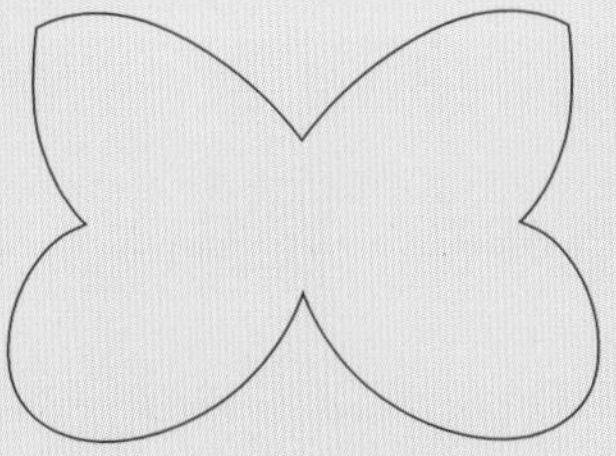

Butterflies in Flight
(see page 60)

diagram B

diagram C

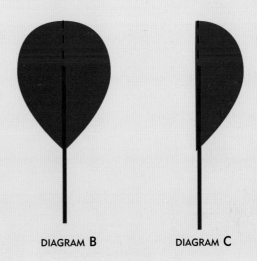

Festive Decorations (see page 70)

diagram D

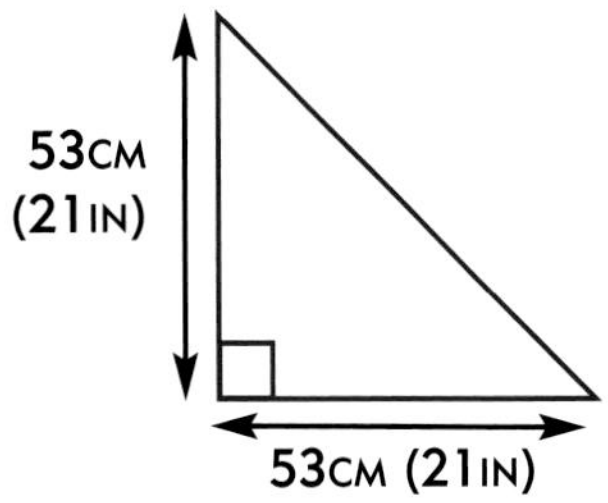
53cm
(21in)
53cm (21in)

Andalusian Headscarf (see page 92)

Designer Motif T-Shirts (see page 96)

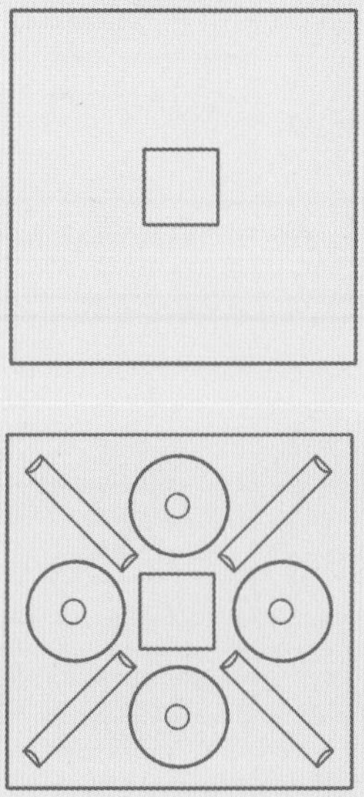

Designer Motif T-Shirts (see page 96)

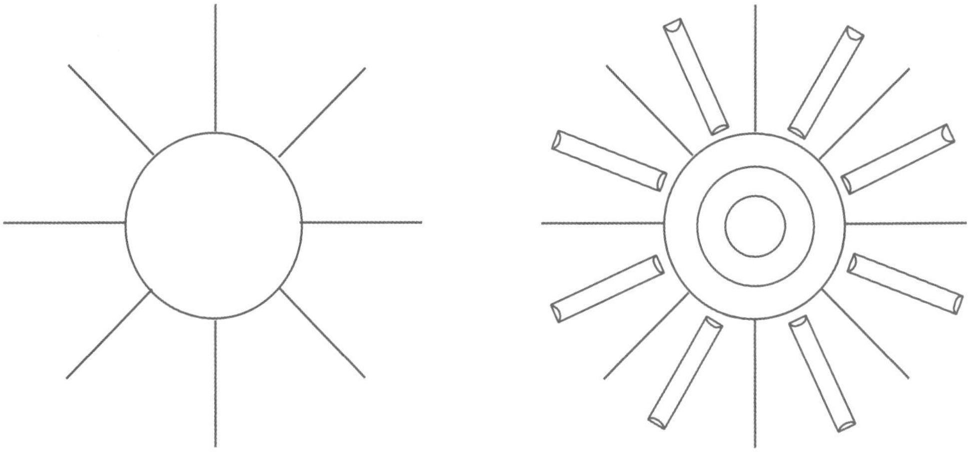

Designer Motif T-Shirts (see page 96)